AF483608

More Than a Game

Finding Grace, Grit and Girlfriends

on the Green

By Dr. Susan Fazio, EdD

Preface

The first time I stood on a tee box with a golf club in my hands, I remember thinking, How hard can this be? That thought lasted about five minutes.

Golf has a way of humbling you almost immediately. The ball doesn't listen. The swing that looked so simple when someone else did it suddenly feels impossibly complicated. And just when you think you're starting to understand the game, it teaches you another lesson in patience.

My husband has been asking me for the past year why I'm writing this book. The answer is simple. I'm writing it for all the new golfers who take up the game and quickly discover, as I did, that golf is much harder than it looks. There were many moments when it would have been easy for me to quit—when the going got rough.

And believe me, the going does get rough. Golf asks a lot of us. It requires patience and focus. It asks us to be bold and courageous. And sometimes it asks us to be willing to look a little foolish.

Hopefully this book offers new golfers encouragement, hope, and a few good reasons to keep going.

My intention is also to open the door to some of the unwritten secrets of the golf world. Many of these things golf professionals never explain, often because they assume everyone already knows them. But beginners don't know them—and they should.

Golf is not a dry, boring sport. It's full of nuance, small discoveries, and moments of joy that keep the game alive and endlessly interesting.

Along the way I share some of the lessons that helped me stay in the game. Many came from my own trial and error. Others came from my girlfriends, who were kind enough to pass along the wisdom they had learned themselves.

And then there is golf etiquette—the part of the game that no one seems to teach you but everyone expects you to understand. For example, ready golf isn't just a suggestion. It's essential if you want everyone in your group—and the people behind you—to enjoy the round.

Like most grandparents, I love watching my grandchildren perform. I enjoy seeing them do gymnastics, play hockey, basketball, and soccer, or appear in school performances. But if I'm honest, what I'd really love is to take them out on the golf course so we can spend real time together.

My hope is that this book opens the door to many enjoyable moments on the course—and helps readers survive the occasional embarrassing ones.

Throughout these pages I share personal stories, not because my experiences are especially important, but because every golfer brings their own stories to the first tee. We carry them with us every time we tee it up. They are part of who we are and part of the fabric of our lives. In the end, that's the real truth about golf.

It's more than a game.

It's a journey filled with laughter, frustration, friendship, and the small triumphs that keep us coming back to the first tee.

More Than a Game is the honest, funny, girlfriend-to-girlfriend guide for women stepping onto the course—whether you're brand new or bravely returning. Sue Fazio picked up a club at 60 and discovered what every woman learns fast: golf is humbling, hilarious, and absolutely worth it.

Inside you'll find:

- **Etiquette without the eye-rolls** — how to be invited back (and actually want to go).
- **Beginner-proof scoring sanity** — Cry Baby Do-Overs, Design Flaws, and other survival tools.
- **Green reading for real people** — from "bucket of water" to AimPoint confidence.
- **Short game, big wins** — the 8-foot practice that changes everything.
- **Mindset that sticks** — one swing thought, not seventeen. Breathe. Pause. Play on.
- **Language decoded** — acronyms, lingo, and the jokes you'll hear on every tee box.
- **Grace under pressure** — because the biggest hazards aren't sand or water; they're in your head.

With stories that will make you laugh (yes, even the mooning-at-17 tale), tips you'll actually use, and a voice that feels like your smartest, kindest friend in the cart, this book will keep you on the course long enough to fall in love with the game—and with the women you play it with.

Come for the golf. Stay for the girlfriends. Leave with a swing, a smile, and a little more courage.

Dedication

I dedicate this book to my husband first. Without his love and patience, I would never have kept going. He's listened to countless rounds of golf by me complete with my perspective on his design "flaws".

Heartfelt thanks to my daughters Jenon, Keegan and Onae for their conversations and love about this project—especially Onae who did the initial editing and endless encouragement and technical guidance. My love and gratitude to my sons Austin and Gavin who ALWAYS try to take care of me and the chaos I create—whether it's printing endless copies of this manuscript or helping me get my game LETTER LAUNCH patented and ready for marketing. I love you all SO MUCH!

I also want to thank my family for supporting my reprioritizing my time to expand to golfing and not babysitting.   And to those seventeen grandchildren who own my heart and are the true reason I've written this book—to show them that life is about commitment and to choose to do what feels right to them and then commit all their energies to making that happen.

And lastly to my girlfriends who've stuck with me on my long golf journey and loving me anyway.

More Than a Game

Finding Grace, Grit and Girlfriends

on the Green

By Susan Fazio, EdD

It's fun to play golf with your husband or partner — there's a comfort there, a shared rhythm and something to talk about over dinner. But there's something special, something essential about playing with other women. Girlfriends bring a whole different kind of energy to the course. There's more laughter, more storytelling, more space to just be yourself.

Contents

Introduction

By Tom Fazio

I tried to talk Sue into playing golf for four decades. This book gives a tiny window into what my wife has accomplished, but I've been there for the past fifty years and it's not the "what" she has done but "how" she has done. What we have in common is passion and commitment to what we agree to do...only Sue does it like a dog with a bone...with such a passion and obsessiveness that it tires most people out. Sue only knows the world of NOW...and so when she took up golf fifteen years ago, she was determined to master the game NOW...unfortunately golf doesn't work that way. She'd be terrible at what I do...I am involved with so many people and so much time to make my "vision" a reality. Sue owns her vision and doesn't expect other people to take part in her vision.

So, when she decided to become a golfer, I took her out and it didn't take long for me to realize she wasn't going to learn golf from me...I suggested taking lessons. She refused. She said she was too embarrassed to swing the club in front of a stranger. So she went to the range and hit thousands of balls until she felt comfortable enough to play with ME. It took years for her to cross over the line to play with other women...more to play with "strange" men. I didn't understand her embarrassment of hitting a bad shot. I told her EVERYONE hits stupid shots...she kept playing and found the secret...GOLF IS A GAME...and she decided to write this book. Obviously, people take years to write a book...she took six months to write her dissertation while raising six kids under the age of nine!

Sue brings all of her passion and commitment to everything she does. When I asked her why she was writing this book (I've written six and it's just headaches and people) and she said (true Sue Fazio) because I wish I would've known what I know now and help gals step into golf with a different mindset...to know golf didn't matter...friendships matter...the real fun part of the game is trying...and being with your girlfriends outside...she's a real outdoorsy person...hiking/kayaking/gardening.

I'm so proud of her as I am of all of her accomplishments. She is my wife, my best friend, mother of my children, an artist, and now...an author. I'm lucky to share the last fifty years with her...now you're lucky to get a glimpse into Sue's world.

Tom Fazio

"Best Modern Day Architect" 3 times by Golf Digest
Over 300 courses in the past 6 decades
Most in Golf Digest's Top 100

When I introduce myself anywhere as "Hi, I'm Sue Fazio."
If they don't take a second take…I know they're not really
into golf. I'm so proud to be his wife.

Beautiful Full Life

Sixteen Grandchildren (Joseph came 2/5/26)

Fore!Word

By Michelle McGann

I've been lucky enough to spend over 30 years on the LPGA Tour playing the game I love at the highest level. Golf has given me a career, a voice, and friendships that have outlasted any trophy I've ever held. But one of the greatest gifts it ever gave me was the chance to meet incredible women like Sue Fazio.

I met Sue about five years ago at a charity event for diabetes. I was diagnosed with Type 1 when I was 13, and starting my foundation was my way of turning something hard into something hopeful. That day, Sue showed up not just to play, but to truly support the cause. We started talking and, honestly, it felt like we'd known each other forever. Then we realized we share the same birthday on December 30th. Just like that, we became "Birthday Buddies."

Since then, we've played together at all sorts of events and shared so many rounds on the course. I've had a front-row seat to Sue's golf journey, and let me tell you, she didn't start out as a natural. She struggled and got frustrated. There were days I'm sure she wanted to quit. But what really stood out to me wasn't her swing or her score. It was her grit. She just kept showing up.

And that's what this book is really about.

I've played with some of the best in the world, including major champions and Hall of Famers. Sue is different. She plays for the love of it. She doesn't play because she's perfect; she plays because she gets what the game gives back.

She didn't pick up a club until later in life. She'd already raised six kids, built a life with her husband Tom, and given so much to her family and community. When she finally stepped onto the course for herself, she brought that same dedication. She practiced. She asked questions. She laughed at her bad shots, and she kept going.

Now, she can walk onto any course with any group and hold her own. But more than that, she brings a kind of joy to the game that's contagious. She plays with heart, with humor, and with gratitude.

Golf has a way of showing you who you really are. It shows how you handle frustration and how you bounce back. It shows whether you cheer for the people next to you. Sue shows up with grace and guts every single time.

She's a beautiful example of what this game can mean for women who are brave enough to try.

This book isn't about being perfect. It's about being brave enough to begin. It's about learning the lingo, the little tricks, the etiquette, and the mindset that help you fall in love with the game. Sue writes the way she plays: honest, warm, and real.

If you're thinking about giving golf a try, consider this your nudge. If you've already started and you're feeling stuck, let this be your pep talk. And if you need proof that it's never too late to start something new, just look at Sue.

She started. She stayed. She loves it. And I have a feeling you will too.

With love,
Michelle McGann
LPGA Professional and Proud Birthday Buddy
7 LPGA Wins 1996 Solheim Cup
Michelle McGann Fund for Diabetes

Michelle is just simply the best person to play golf with in my world. I'm humbled that she plays with me. But it doesn't feel embarrassing...it feels like friends doing something REAL together. I love her.

Fore!Word

By Nancy Lopez

I was fortunate to learn golf from my father. From the time I was a young girl, he took me to municipal golf courses and taught me the game. When I won my first tournament at eight years old, I was hooked.

But the most important thing my dad ever taught me about golf had nothing to do with mechanics. It had to do with attitude. He always told me to think positive and to play happy. That simple philosophy stayed with me throughout my entire career.

Two years ago, I spent some time with Sue at the Masters during a social event. As we talked, I quickly realized she shared the same positive outlook about golf that my father believed in. When she told me she was writing a book for women who are taking up the game later in life, I was delighted to support her project.

Encouraging women to enjoy the game of golf is something I care deeply about. Through my Nancy Lopez Golf Adventures program, along with LPGA professionals

Sue Powers and Teresa Zamboni, we travel around the world teaching and playing golf with women who love the game.

Women spend so much of their lives taking care of others. Golf offers something special — a chance to unplug from daily obligations, step away from technology, enjoy the beauty of the outdoors, and recharge. Sometimes the best advice is to leave your phone on mute, except for emergencies, and simply enjoy the round.

And remember, when you hit a bad shot, don't let it affect the next one. My father always told me, "If you have a backswing, you have a chance." That advice applies to every golfer.

Everyone struggles when they first begin playing golf. Don't get discouraged. Take lessons early from a golf professional and give yourself time to learn.

Sue's book offers encouragement, humor, and practical advice for beginners, along with helpful tips that even experienced players will appreciate. Most of all, it captures the joy that golf can bring into your life.

I hope you'll become as hooked on golf as Sue has and discover all the wonderful things this game has to offer.

Because golf truly is more than just a game.

Nancy Lopez

LPGA Hall of Fame

48 LPGA Tour Victories

Nancy Lopez Golf Adventures

(nancylopezgolfadventures.com)

Nancy has always been my golf inspiration and then hero and then friend.

Fore!Word

By Meredith Elliot Powell

Golf - Friendship- The Love of The Game

Sue and I have been friends for more than thirty years, becoming fast and lifelong friends over a botched backpacking trip. That's another story for another book.

When I first met Sue, she did not play golf, nor did she have any interest in the game. We spent our time together hiking, volunteering in our community, and taking part listening to the various spiritual leaders that would visit our little area of the country.

It was not until Sue's last child left for college that Sue decided to pick up a club. I was so intrigued when she told me not only that she was going to start playing, but what her approach was going to be.

See it was not that she really wanted to play golf, nor did she have a deep desire to learn the game. But she knew with all six children gone, and husband whose only interest was golf; it was time to learn. So much wisdom in that lesson.

I was also intrigued by her approach. For one year, she would hit 100 golf balls every single day. Not because she wanted to, or because she loved to, but because Sue knew to learn to play this game, it would take discipline, commitment, and a life-long dedication to learning. Again, so much wisdom in that lesson.

Over the years Sue has not only learned to love the game, but become obsessed with it, I have gone on this journey with her. We have played in countless member guest tournaments, traveled to beautiful courses, and made a deep friendship even stronger all through the shared love of golf.

Golf is that rare sport that can be enjoyed by young and old, where people not at the same skill level can always play together, and a sport that gives back to you far more than you ever invest in the game.

Meredith Elliot Powell

Hall of Fame Speaker

Best Selling Author

Business Growth Strategist

Meredith and I have hiked in many places. We attempted to walk the Appalachian Trail in the Blue Ridge Mountains up to Maine…we didn't make it…it built our friendship when we both said "uncle" at the same time. We've hiked the Dolomite Mountains with Backroads Company and had many crazy disasters along the way beginning with Meredith starting with food poisoning on the train to start our adventure. We've now become members of USSWGA and that's been a great honor to belong to together. I've stood by in awe as she's created a mind-boggling career in public speaking that takes her all over the world. We play in many member guest tournaments basically because we just like spending time together FIRST, golf second.

Author's Note

<hr>

Note to the Men (and a Heads-Up for the Ladies):

Husbands, do **not** buy this book for your wife if she's been playing golf since she was a kid. She won't appreciate it—and she doesn't need it.

Boyfriends, same goes for you: if your girlfriend is a single-digit handicapper, she's already got the game. This book isn't for her.

This book is for the women who are *finally* stepping onto the course—after decades of raising kids, running households, caretaking, working full-time, or playing tennis. Now, they've carved out space for something new. For something just for them. They're going to finally do it.

This book is for you, ladies.

It's for those who think they'll *"try"* golf...and then quickly realize:

Golf is HARD.

This book is here to keep you in the game. To help you laugh when you want to quit. To remind you that you're not alone—and that it's okay to swing and miss (again and again).

Because you'll quickly discover:

Golf is more than a game.

I wrote this book because I believe how you do anything is how you do everything. So, what I do/say all of the time is...THE TRUTH IS. My friends hear that from me. My children. My husband. It's just my bottom line, I guess. My signature phrase. One day when I was in my thirties, a book was delivered to my house—no return address—no one took the credit for sending it to this day. *THE TRUTH IS.* It was written by Sri H.W.L. Poonja. It is a collection of words spoken by Sri H.W.L. Poonja during gatherings with his students in north India between 1990 and 1997. It resonated with me when I received the book which I have read cover to cover. So, me and Poonja... *The Truth Is*...so this is another in my personal chapter of *The Truth Is* as relates to golf.

There's a lot of difference between men and women on the golf course...now that's an understatement...but it's not just physical and mental—

it's emotional. Just like the book *MEN ARE FROM MARS AND WOMEN ARE FROM VENUS*—they process things differently. Let's say there are two men as partners playing in a tournament…the first shanks it into the water. The second guy gets up and is thinking "I'm going to hit the longest shot in my life right up there on the green." He's thinking he's going to be the hero.

For beginning women golfers in that same situation, the thought process might sound more like "oh no—now it's all on me and I don't want to let my partner down."

Obviously, this is not ALL men and ALL women. Women are not wrong to think/feel that way. HOWEVER the men's positive attitude is much more optimistic and appropriate on the golf course…maybe they have more golf courses on Mars than Venus.

Chapter 1: What Took Me So Long?

"You've got to believe in yourself,
and you've got to keep trying"
-Babe Didrikson Zaharias

———————————
———————————
———————————

This book is for all the girls who have been too busy working, raising kids, taking care of projects, and who finally have found some time to lift up their heads from all of those commitments and are looking for a way to spend some time away from the obligations they have. It's for those who may have friends, family, or husbands who have been playing golf for a long time and encourage them to take up the game. These girls have spent countless hours listening to their partners, fathers, and friends recounting the moments of their rounds on the golf course.

These girls have listened patiently to stories about the balls that "almost went in for a hole in one" and the outrageous audacity of the balls that "went to the beach," (sand trap/bunkers). It's sorta like listening to fisherman about the "10-pound fish that got away. Politely and tirelessly, the gals have listened to outrageous stories.

I heard a great tale before I started playing about the guy from a famous course who was to be a potential member of this prestigious club. It was a par three. He hits the ball and it's a blind shot, (meaning the four guys can't see the green or where the ball went) and the guy and everyone looks for the ball. The man who hit the ball "finds" it behind the green. He says, "I found it!" and hit it. Unfortunately, a partner finds his original ball in the hole. Needless to say, not only did that gentleman not get credit for his hole in one; he was escorted off the course and was not invited back. Oh, the tragedy. How ridiculous it is to hear about random people playing a random game when you've never played.

Golf is a game of honor and respect. The gals who don't golf hear this over and over. These conversations are incredibly interesting to golfers, not so much to people who don't play the game. I used to think to myself, of course, these people have spent four hours of their lives playing a game, and now another eight hours talking about the game. That's sorta crazy don't you think?

This book is for you if you have a golf addict in your life. It seems they watch people play this "boring" game more than they play! You have spent countless Sundays with your golfer, glued to the TV watching other people play golf. Like The Masters Week. For golfers, that is like the holy week. Everything stops. In our house, no one is allowed to talk while the addict is glued to the set. They appreciate food brought to them but not conversation.

And that's where I spent my honeymoon 50 years ago. My husband is THE Tom Fazio - #1 golf course architect with over 31 courses in the top 200 (the next on the list only has 14). He's designed over 300 golf courses around the world during his sixty-year career. He KNOWS golf. Your golfer knows who he is. And that honeymoon weekend, 50 years ago, he figured he could do a twofer - get married AND do The Masters tournament in Augusta, Georgia. Well, until I met Tom, I had never known a golfer. I had never touched a golf ball. I had never heard of the Masters golf tournament let alone that it is the gold standard for all other tournaments. It's the only major in golf consistently played in the same venue every year. So, when Tom suggested that we go there for a honeymoon, I thought, why not?

Well, this was before he was "TOM FAZIO." We did not have a reservation. He was 30 years old and he was taking care of the details of the honeymoon. I took care of the wedding. Fair game. So, we drove into Augusta, GA on April 5, 1975, with no reservations. We roll into town and Tom pulls into The Alamo Hotel and books a room. The key fob says, "NOT RESPONSIBLE FOR PERSONAL INJURY OR PROPERTY DAMAGE." The room had chipped linoleum tile, a nasty stain on the chenille bedspread, and a shower curtain divided the bathroom from the bedroom. We walked right out of that "honeymoon suite," —our honeymoon was off to a great start. We got to the tournament and Tom had a clubhouse badge; I had a general admission ticket and an umbrella. Tom told me to meet him by "The Tree" at noon, and he'd go with me around the course— he had some business to attend to and some hands to shake. No big deal, I thought.

Barbara Nicklaus had a similar story when Jack stopped by Pine Valley Golf Club (an all men's club) on their honeymoon while Barbara sat in the car and was driven around the perimeter—she never played golf after that either.

People ask me why it took me so long to take up golf since I married the number one golf course architect in the history of the game. Well, that honeymoon is the beginning reason. And then we had six children in nine years. We met and got married in Jupiter, Florida and gave birth to all of our children there. We then moved to North Carolina when the youngest, Gavin, was two weeks old. We moved to a farm because I was raised on one in Ohio, and that seemed much more logical raising kids in nature instead of the hustle and bustle and HEAT of South Florida. We had horses and chickens and goats and a garden. And while we knew no one there, the kids kept me plenty busy. I raised the children vegetarian.

Tom flew out on Mondays and came home on Fridays. When he came home on Fridays, we'd have pizza with the kids. Tom would 'fold into' our family life which admittedly was chaotic with horses and goats and chickens. Then on Saturday night we'd go to a movie, dinner and go bowling. After about four months of this Tom asked, "Is this it Sue…just you and me?" Well, I had no idea how to make friends in this community, so my answer was, "Well yes…you/me and these six children…"

I was intimately involved with their school. I worked on my dissertation and received a doctorate. I taught 4th grade social studies at their small elementary school and was the counselor for four years, was PTA president, etc. The kids, Jenon, Logan, Keegan, Austin, Onae and Gavin, were taking Suzuki violin, ballet, jazz, soccer, football, basketball, baseball, more basketball, you name it. We were BUSY. I drove a 15-passenger white Dodge van. It only made sense.

Tom and I started The Boys and Girls Club in our town of Hendersonville in 1993, eight years after we moved there, because you know, I wasn't busy enough! There was a real need to help the youth in our town, and we were blessed to be able to do it. It has been our proudest achievement besides raising our children. I was an adjunct professor at UNCA for three years. I was intimately involved with The Boys and Girls Club and still am 31 years later. I started a paint your own pottery business on Main Street called the Blue Butterfly Studio and had a "Fruity Rooty Juice Bar." I worked there five days a week.

My parents moved to Hendersonville and needed care and attention. We designed and built an 11,000 square foot home with a mile long driveway. We had a lot of parties, fun times, horses, goats, rabbits and a 40' teepee. I bought a motorhome and took the kids two summers in a row across the country without Tom. He would fly into the big cities and we'd meet him.

We had adventures every day. One night in December when there was 1' of snow on the ground, our horse fell into the swimming pool. It was covered with a tarpaulin-type cover, so it was covered with snow. Tom tells me to go call someone—we had no friends. It took three exhausting, nerve-racking hours to get her out. We even had a bear break into the house. The oldest Jenon was returning home, and a bear was sitting on the front porch eating the apples that I kept in a tub on the front porch. Jenon screamed—the bear jumps up and blasts through the glass front door into the room where the rest of the kids were watching TV. Jenon went right in after to save the five kids. So, you see—I was never bored or lonely. It took Tom a whole year to figure out I was staying in North Carolina. He finally opened an office in Hendersonville.

One by one, the kids graduated, went to college, got married, and moved. So, all of this is why I didn't take up golf until I was 60 even though it was the constant in our life. I just couldn't. Not yet.

Many and most women are too busy like I was to take up and commit to golf. So, this book is for all of you, my girlfriends who are struggling to figure out, "Why am I doing this?" So when asked why it took me so long to take up golf, my advice right now is: if you still don't have time to commit to hitting balls (not necessarily play golf) at least 3 times a week, please wait to begin. It's not quite your time yet. You MUST have time to practice!

When we became empty nesters, I looked at Tom and thought: we needed to do something together, so we have something to talk about. All the obligations of child raising shifted into a new phase. A very different life, needless to say. I was still plenty busy. I'm an artist and I paint every day. And now I'm addicted to pottery, so I still have plenty to do. I have an obsession with flowers that consumes hours and hours and brings me so much joy. I am grateful to have many friends, and we hike, kayak, play rummikub cards—DO THINGS…I thought, well, I love to go to the movies, I love to travel, see different places. Tom does none of those things.

So, golf it is. A no brainer. I'd been circling around the vortex of golf for 35 years, I might as well surrender to its pull.

It doesn't take too long to find out the real truth about golf though:

GOLF IS HARD.

> There's so many rules. There's so many thoughts. Head down/ don't move your eyes/ shift your weight/ bellybutton to the hole/ relax/ butt out/ left arm straight/ hold your finish/ left shoulder up/ right shoulder down when addressing the ball. AND THERE'S ONLY ONE PROPER WAY TO GRIP THE CLUB. Don't lift the club/ weight on balls of the feet/ follow through high if you want the ball to land soft/ left hand flat against the sky/ backswing weight inside feet/ follow through is low to have the ball run. All of these swing thoughts were just my first lesson. Oh, the overload.

When I first played with Tom, I'd swing, and he'd point out which of the swing thoughts I did not execute properly. "You were too fast, you picked up the club, you picked up your head, you decelerated at the ball, you swayed...etc. etc. etc." and that was before I learned what a reverse pivot was.

And we weren't even talking about putting the ball...that's a whole different set of suggestions. (See Chapter 7) Rock your shoulder/ keep head down until you hear the ball drop in the cup/ hold the club like a bird's tongue/ slow back/ equal forward/ look at the hole/ look at the ball/ drag the putter back slowly/ bring the putter back through. Putting has a science of its own.

So, there I found myself—at 60 years old, finally picking up a club after decades of diapers, deadlines, and dinner duty. Not because I needed something to do, but because I finally had space to do something just for me— and maybe, just maybe, with my husband.

Golf didn't come naturally. It came with frustration, confusion, and a whole lot of swing thoughts. But it also came with laughter, fresh air, and the unexpected joy of trying something continuously hard— and doing it anyway.

If you're just starting your golf journey—or even just *thinking* about starting—this book is for you. I've walked the long road to the tee box for the past 15 years, and I'm here to say: the view's pretty great once you get there.

LET'S PLAY!

Chapter 2: The History of Women's Golf:
A Game Fit for a Queen

"The best advice I ever got was to keep swinging and enjoy the game" -Mickey Wright

You've heard my story of how I went from never touching a golf ball, to marrying a golf course architect, to being too busy to pick up a club, and finally, at 60 years old, stepping into the game. To say golf is central to my life would be an understatement. I credit it with building deep friendships, strengthening my marriage, keeping me physically active and fit, and sustaining me mentally and emotionally. It's not a small thing, and it's precisely why I'm writing this book. I want that for my daughters, my granddaughters, and you!

At first, I saw golf as something that took my husband away—those long weeks without him, his obsession with course design, the quiet hours of tinkering and talking. But over time I saw it differently: as a healthy, meaningful sport and lifestyle. We talk all the time about how this game has been a game changer for us. A lifestyle I eventually fell in love with. But if it became part of my life later in life, why are so many women shy to take it up early? Why has golf long felt like a men's domain?

I started digging into the history. What I found was surprising, inspiring—and sometimes frustrating. Because the story of women in golf is one of determination, exclusion, pioneering spirit, and gradual triumph.

Mary, Queen of Scots (1542–1567)

Believe it or not, the first recorded female golfer is Mary, Queen of Scotland. She ruled Scotland from 1542 to 1567, and it was during her reign that the famous St. Andrews Links golf course was built. I've actually played this course-two times, how cool. It is a beautiful, challenging course.

A queen with a driver? I love that. Let that be your image when being out there on the course. If you get the opportunity to play St. Andrew's, DO THAT! You don't have to be "good enough" to play St. Andrews. It's an experience you won't want to miss because it's so very different from all of the American golf courses. It has eight shared fairways where two different holes run alongside or cross over! It has seven shared or double greens!! The Swilcan Burn (a hairy ditch which is a drainage channel) runs across the 1st and 18th fairways. Bring extra balls! The Hell Bunker is on the 14th hole which when I was in it meant I STAYED IN IT until I bent over and picked up the ball and walked out with my head hung low...the wind is really the hidden hazard and becomes the slap of nature that throws your ball wherever she wants to!

Back then, golf was simpler with fewer rules, rougher courses, but the image of a woman wielding a club in 1560 is powerful, isn't it? A game fit for a queen, indeed. Legend has it, we can thank her for the word "caddie." She called her helpers "cadets," and over time, the name stuck—because of course it did. Queens start trends.

The Early Barriers

Over the centuries, golf evolved. But by the 19th century, it became formalized, codified, and exclusive. Golf clubs emerged with strict membership rules. Women were often relegated to Sundays or peripheral status. Many clubs barred women entirely—or allowed them only in limited capacities: as guests, for social events, or in unscheduled tee times.

In 1894, the Ladies' Golf Union (LGU) was formed in the UK, offering women a governing body and their own championships. (Let us give praise to the early champions—Issette Pearson, Violet Henry, May Hezlet). Over in the U.S., the U.S. Women's Amateur

Championship started in 1895. Women were saying: we play too.

Still, even with these institutions, women's golf was overshadowed, marginalized, and often underfunded. Travel was harder, social norms dissuaded athletic competitiveness in women, and full professional circuits would take much longer to emerge. There are maybe a half dozen all-men golf courses in America—no all women! At our home course, Jupiter Hills in Florida, our ladies golf association has 256 members.

The Mid-20th Century: Pioneers and Progress

As the 1900s progressed, women fought for more access. Names you might recognize: Babe Didrikson Zaharias—an Olympic champion who helped legitimize women's competitive golf; Louise Suggs, Marlene Hagge, and Betty Jameson—who, along with ten others, founded the LPGA in 1950. These women were not only champions; they were builders.

The Ladies Professional Golf Association was a radical step. In its early days, tournaments were small, purses were modest, and travel was grueling. These women crisscrossed the country in station wagons, sharing hotel rooms, equipment, and ambition. They weren't just playing for trophies; they were carving out space for every woman who would ever pick up a club.

And here's where I smile every time I think about it: I was born that same year—1950. Maybe it's coincidence, maybe it's serendipity, but I like to think I arrived just as women's golf was taking a bold new swing. While those pioneers were teeing up the future, I was taking my first breath—destined, it seems, to fall in love with a man spearheading the building of courses and this game decades later.

Maybe that's the beauty of women's golf: no matter when you start, you're already part of something historic.

In the decades since, women's golf has grown in visibility, sponsorship, and opportunity—though inequality still exists. For example: prize money gaps, fewer televised events, fewer club facilities for women, and lingering stereotypes that golf is a man's game.

Nancy Lopez: A New Kind of Champion

By the late 1970s, US women's golf had its first true superstar in Nancy Lopez. With her easy smile, fierce focus, and unmistakable swing, she made golf feel approachable. She wasn't just winning tournaments; she was changing perceptions. Fans loved her because she played with heart and humanity. She brought family, femininity, and joy to a sport that often took itself a little too seriously.

But here's the funny part—I wasn't paying attention back then. I didn't follow men's golf let alone women's golf, and I didn't watch Nancy Lopez win her tournaments. I didn't realize what she was doing for the game or for women like me who would one day fall in love with it. I was living life, raising a family, doing everything but watching golf.

And then, years later, life being what it is, I met Nancy in person. She happened to be a good friend of one of our friends, and suddenly there she was—this woman whose legacy I hadn't appreciated when it was unfolding. Meeting her felt like the universe's gentle wink, a reminder that sometimes the people and passions meant for us have a way of circling back in their own time.

What I love most is that Nancy is still doing what she's always done—making golf more welcoming for women. She's created a club just for women to start playing, building the same sense of belonging that she embodied throughout her career. She even has a golf course in The Villages, Florida, that carries her name—another space where women can gather, learn, and play without intimidation.

When I think of her now, I see not just a champion, but a connector. She continues to open doors for women who may not yet realize that they belong on the course too. Her joy was contagious then, and it still is now. She's proof that when women rise in golf, they lift the entire game

She's created a Nancy Lopez golf adventures organization. She accompanies the guests along with two female pros and takes them to different destinations where they play golf and explore. This year they are going to Ireland and then Iceland! Check out her website, nancylopezgolfadventures.com!

What It Means for Us Now

When I began playing later in life, I didn't think about the women who came before me. I didn't even consider it. I was too in my head about how hard the game was—how impossible it felt to make clean contact, to stay patient, to not throw my club in the pond. I was self-conscious and beating myself up about how awful I was. I wasn't thinking about trailblazers; I was just trying to get the ball in the air. I found myself holding my breath when addressing the ball (that's what we do when we are afraid). IT DOESN'T HELP!

But looking back, I see it differently now. Every fairway I walked, every league I joined, every time I felt welcome on a course—it was because someone before me fought for that space. Someone was told no and kept showing up anyway.

At the time, I didn't realize I was carrying forward layers of struggle and opportunity built by countless women before me. When I hit my first good shot, I thought it was all me. Now I know: I'm playing because she paid the price.

So, here's what I want for every woman reading this: I want you to play golf because they made it possible. I want you to step onto the course knowing you belong there. I want you to take up space in this arena joyfully, boldly, and unapologetically. Be a Queen.

About five years ago I met Michelle McGann when I was invited to play in her charity event to raise funds and awareness for diabetes. At 13 she was diagnosed with Type 1 diabetes. She was born on my birthday — December 30 — in the year I graduated from high school, 1969. She is a 3-time Florida State Junior Champion, the 1987 USGA Junior Girls Champion, the AJGA Rolex Junior Player of the Year, Rolex Junior First-team All-American, and the 1988 Doherty Cup championship. Since joining the LPGA, she has won 8 professional tournaments and participated in two Solheim Cups. There are other wins and honors in her career but now I have had the joy of playing with her several times.

She's always gracious and fun to play with and never tells me what I'm doing wrong but will kindly help me read a putt if asked (and ONLY then-very unlike my husband who is always trying to be helpful). She's shared many unique stories about her career, like the time she was in a tournament and had a fifteen on the first hole and went on to win the whole tournament. I always try to remember that when I screw up my first hole in a tournament— *don't give up*!

She's my Birthday Buddy but so much more— she's the face I pull up in my memory when I need a pep talk. Her smile is huge and contagious...remember that when you're playing in a tournament: IT'S NOT ALL ABOUT YOU!!! You're affecting everyone in your foursome— be a joyous, encouraging reflection of the privilege of playing this game! Give God thanks that you're healthy enough and connected enough to be on a golf course!

Because golf isn't just about mastering a skill; it's about continuing a story. Every time we tee off, we declare: I belong here. Every laugh, every mishit, every shot you chase—you're not just playing a game. You're honoring a legacy.

Looking Ahead

I don't want to rewrite all the pages of history here; you'll find there's a mountain of stories, clubs, tours, and battles. But I want you to see that you're entering into something much bigger than your swing. You are part of this history, this light, this delight.

So, when you grip that club, glance down the fairway, feel the weight in your hands—know this: women have been doing this for centuries. Some in modest gardens, some against odds. You are not late. You are not late at all.

Modern Women, Modern Wins, and the Wild Characters I've Met Along the Way

Here's something I always think about when it comes to women's golf: the progress is real, but the gap is still enormous — financially, culturally, and in visibility.

Just look at the **money**.

- The **highest-earning male golfer of all time** is **Tiger Woods**, with $121 million in career winnings…and lifetime career earnings of $1.8 billion (prize money + endorsements).

- The **highest-earning female golfer** is **Annika Sörenstam**, with about **$22 million** in career winnings.

Read that again:

$1,800,000,000 versus $22,000,000.

Same sport.

Same number of holes.

Same size of cup.

But a vastly different opportunity.

And yet — women play.

Women persist.

And women keep making space.

I know some of them personally, and they are amazing humans first, golfers second.

The Perks (and Perils) of Being Married to Tom Fazio

Because I married Tom Fazio, I have met more professional golfers than I ever imagined I would — often without knowing who they were until after I made a fool of myself.

One time, I was at an event, talking with a man named **Billy**. I didn't know who he was. We had a long conversation, and at some point, I said — very sincerely — "Golfers are pretty simple-minded, you know? I've had so many boring conversations with golfers. You don't seem to be boring at all. How often do you play?"

He said, very politely, "Pretty often."

He was at my dinner table that night.

So you can imagine my shock when he got up on stage to introduce **Jack Nicklaus** — because he was **Billy Andrade**, a four-time PGA Tour winner, Ryder Cup vice-captain, and member of the Golf Hall of Fame.

I felt like a complete idiot.

But, somehow, we became good friends after that.

The Putting Lesson Disaster (That Still Haunts Me)

Then there's **Brad Faxon** — widely considered the greatest putter in the history of golf.

One year at The Masters, he stayed at the same house as Tom and me. I didn't know who he was, and Tom asked him to show me how he putts.

Brad picked up a putter in the living room, demonstrated his technique, and — I kid you not — I corrected him.

I said, "Brad, that's not the right way to putt."

Yes.

I said that to Brad Faxon.

Now, every year, we work together on a fundraising tournament for Jupiter Medical Center — Tom and Brad are the co-chairs — and every time Brad gets up to speak, he tells the room:

"I just want everyone to know that Sue Fazio taught me how to putt."

Imagine that.

Tom Watson, the Burn, and the Hairy Tits

The first time I met **Tom Watson** — who I actually did watch and admire — he was my dinner partner.

And I had just played Kiawah Island Club: **Cacique**, one of his courses.

So I asked, very innocently:

"Tom, why didn't you pipe that creek on the first hole? That parallel hazard — you know, that's a terrible idea."

He said, "I put that creek there. It's a burn — like in Scotland."

I said, "Right, but in Scotland they didn't have the equipment to cover it up."

Then I said, "And what about the hairy tits on the back of 18? They don't do that in Ireland, either."

He looked at me with a completely blank face.

Tom — my Tom — had a LOT to say to me afterward.

And Tom Watson turned his chair around and stopped talking to me completely.

Lesson learned: Men can also be very sensitive about what they create.

Jupiter Hills: From Embarrassment to Belonging

The first time I played Ladies Day at Jupiter Hills, I was clearly the **D player** — thirty-something handicap — paired with an A player, probably an eight.

I was so nervous I played even worse than usual.

By the third hole, she turned around and said, "Are you sure you're married to Tom Fazio?"

I said, "Aren't we on the same team? Is that supposed to help me play better?"

Now we play together often and laugh about it every time.

That's the thing about women in golf — we don't forget, but we forgive.

A Little Trick from Me to You

Whenever I'm on the green during a tournament, I say: **"I'm here in three — what's everyone else lying?"**

It's a friendly way of keeping the game honest.

In golf, "lying" has nothing to do with morals. No one is being accused of anything. It simply means how many shots it took you to get onto the green.

So when I say, "I'm here in five—what's everyone else lying?" I'm not starting an interrogation. I'm just letting everyone know how many shots it took me to arrive and inviting the group to quietly compare notes *before* we start putting. It avoids mysterious math later and prevents that end-of-round conversation that always begins with,

"Wait... how did you get a five?" If someone disagrees, we just walk through how we got there. And then everyone putts—aware, accountable, and in integrity.

Golf can be serious, but it doesn't have to be secretive.

If you're playing in a tournament, you're often asked to exchange scorecards. This protects the field and guards against what I like to call *faulty memories*. Just last year, I played in a Member-Guest where the pros told us to exchange cards on the first tee. When we tried, the other team refused. What were we going to do—arm wrestle them?

So, we quietly kept their score anyway, just to honor the spirit of the game. When the cards were turned in, they posted two fewer strokes than we had recorded. They made the playoff—but the Golf Gods had opinions, and they didn't advance.

The lesson?

Honesty matters in this game.

Exchanging scorecards keeps things clean, fair, and drama-free—exactly how golf is meant to be played.

Why This Matters

Women don't just play golf.

We **build community**.

We **raise money**.

We **show up sick and still finish the round**.

We **accidentally insult legends**,

and then become friends.

We **take up space — with humor and heart.**

And I always think:

We are still catching up to the financial rewards — but in spirit, generosity, and grit, I wouldn't trade places with the men for anything. Women belong in this game.

Chapter 3: Golf Etiquette: How to Get People to Ask You to Play Again

"Success in golf depends less on strength of body than upon strength of mind and character." -Arnold Palmer

Let's be real. Golf is already challenging. The last thing you want is to accidentally break an unspoken rule and become *that girl*—the one people politely tolerate, but never invite again. Golf can be intimidating at first.

This chapter is your guide to what no one tells you but assumes you know it when you start playing: the quiet language, invisible rules, and tiny habits that make the golf experience enjoyable—for you and everyone else in your foursome.

Be Ready to Play "Ready Golf."

This is an outdoor sport. Be prepared for it all: rain, cold, wind, hunger, thirst, bugs, blazing sun, and headaches. Seriously. Bring the Advil, bring the bug spray, toss in a protein bar, and don't forget sunscreen, lip balm, a towel, maybe even a band-aid or two.

Your golf bag is big enough to carry more than just clubs—think of it as your on-course survival kit. Also, IF there's any chance of rain–bring a rain suit complete with rain gloves and hat.

Ready Golf isn't just about pace—it's about presence. You're *ready* to hit when it's your turn. You're *ready* for whatever the day throws at you, from sudden weather changes to your fifth chunked shot in a row. You're *ready* to laugh it off, take a deep breath, and keep going. Being mentally, emotionally and physically prepared helps you enjoy the game (and helps your playing partners enjoy *you*). It's the kind of readiness that keeps the round moving, the energy light, and the invite list open.

Now, if you're reading this, you probably want to play. And maybe you've practiced enough on the range to build a little confidence—but you're still afraid of embarrassing yourself. You don't want to be terrible. But even if you are, it doesn't mean you're a terrible person. Your dog still loves you.

I'm a painter first, and one of my favorite lessons came from a teacher who said: *"There's no such thing as a bad painting—just a painting that's not done yet."*

Well, guess what? You're not done as a golfer, no matter how many shots you mess up. Keep going. Keep swinging. You'll get it. Here's a step by step of how to get through your day at the golf course.

Before You Tee Off: Pre-Round Vibes

Arrive early. Not obnoxiously early, but early enough to check in, stretch, swing a few clubs, maybe roll a few putts. Golf isn't the place to come screeching into the parking lot with your shoes half on and Starbucks in hand. Use the bathroom. Trust me on this one.

Hit the Range (or at Least Swing at Something)

Let's talk about practice shots, the warm-up kind. You don't need to wear yourself out before the round even begins, but a little time on the range goes a long way—especially if you're trying to avoid that awkward first tee shank. (And if you're wondering what a *shank* is—it's when you hit the ball with the wrong part of the club, and it shoots off sideways like it's trying to escape the course. Trust me, you don't want to start your round that way.)

If you've got 15 extra minutes, go hit a small bucket of balls. Start with a wedge or short iron...don't pull out the driver first. Hit a few shots with each club you think you'll use. Focus more on rhythm than results. You're not trying to fix your swing—you're just waking up your muscles and reminding your body what it's here to do. Remember you will only use your driver 14 times max— so practice those chips and putts proportionally more!

And if there's a practice putting green nearby, go roll a few. Don't skip this part. You'll get a feel for the speed of the greens—and even if you have no idea what you're doing, people will think you do. (Which is half of the battle.) One of the best tips someone gave me is: find a level hole to putt to and assume your putting stance–bring your putter back to your right foot (if you're a right hander) and move it to your left foot while hitting the ball. Do this 3 times and then step off the distance...you will use this measurement to judge the speed of the putt. If you have a putt that distance while on the course, use that measurement (toe to toe) —more or less, considering whether it is downhill or uphill, further or shorter.

Even five solid minutes with a club in your hand before the round makes a difference. Think of it like stretching before a dance class. You're telling your body,

"Hey, we're about to do something weird and elegant and occasionally frustrating. Let's warm up first."

So yes, practice shots matter. Not because they guarantee a good round—but because they help you start feeling like a golfer before you've even hit the first tee. And that confidence? That's worth at least three strokes.

On the Tee Box

This is where you officially enter the world of golf. It's sacred turf—literally. Stand quietly when others are hitting. Don't rattle tees or whisper to your girlfriend. Stay still. Even movement in their peripheral vision can throw someone off.

Who hits first? Usually, the person with the best score on the last hole (called "having honors"). But among girlfriends, just ask: "Want me to go?" You're not at the PGA. You're just trying to get the ball in the air. It's called READY GOLF.

On the first tee, get out of the cart, stand by the tee, and be ready. Use your rangefinder (you need one of these, or newer golf carts have the technology to show you) and know your distance while you wait. On par 3s take the club to the ball that goes that distance from the cart and take that club to the ball.

The easiest way to know the distance your clubs go is to go to a track man (at a training center) and hit each club in your bag and write that distance down for the club and create a cheat sheet that you put in your bag for reference). If the wind is with you use less club— against you use more.

If you FEEL the wind on your face it's one club. If you HEAR the wind it's two . You can't take that to the bank but it will give you confidence to help decide which club is most appropriate. If the wind is against you and you usually set up with that club closer to the front of your stance— move it back an inch— it will have less lift. If the wind is with you move it an inch forward from your normal stance and let the wind lift the ball up and take it further.

If the ball has an uphill lie take a longer club (like a 6 rather than a 7). If your ball is on a downhill lie take less club because you need more loft (like an 8 rather than a 7).

Watch your partner's shot. Say something positive AFTER it lands. Nothing is more frustrating than if you say "good shot" and the ball lands in a bunker or out of bounds.

If you see a snake or animal on the course do not shriek…it might be in the middle of the person's swing on the next hole. If it's a skunk BACK UP! It'd be a good story but a stinky one.

Pace of Play

It's not a rule in golf but a courtesy to not have more than two practice swings in your pre-shot routine. No more than two practice swings...I've been with women who take six or seven — doesn't mean they'll hit better. It is just annoying the gals around them who want to hit their ball!!

The number one reason people love—or avoid—playing with someone is pace of play. Golf can be slow, but it shouldn't be glacial.

Be ready when it's your turn. Don't wait until everyone else has hit to start looking for your club.

Lost a ball? Look for no more than 3 minutes, then drop one and keep going. Everyone has lost a ball. Everyone appreciates someone who doesn't take it personally.

On the Green

The green is like a temple. Walk gently, don't step in anyone's putting line (the imaginary line between their ball and the hole), and don't talk when someone's putting. Don't move around when someone is ready to putt.

Pro tip: when someone sinks a long putt, you can say "great putt." If they miss a short one—say nothing. Just...silence.

Also, if you're the first to finish putting, offer to pick up the flagstick or tend it. It's a small gesture that speaks volumes.

You're *ready*.

Take Care of the Course

Replace divots, rake bunkers, fix ball marks. It's like cleaning up after yourself at a friend's house—you may not live there, but you're a guest.

Golf courses are beautiful, sacred, and expensive to maintain. Leave them better than you found them.

Golf Carts & Good Energy

Don't be the cart chaos driver. Drive responsibly. Golf carts are designed to ride on cart paths or on fairways. Avoid driving in the roughs except to get to the fairways. The reason you do this is to not mash the rough down. Park behind or to the side of greens, not in front.

Bring good energy. Golf can be frustrating. We all top shots, miss short putts, and occasionally launch a ball into a pond. Shake it off. Laugh. Don't apologize the whole time. Just breathe and swing again. A positive attitude will take you the whole way through your game.

When in Doubt, Ask

New to the game? Ask questions. Most golfers love sharing knowledge, as long as you're respectful and trying to learn. Say: "Is it okay if I do this?" or "What's the rule here?" People appreciate someone who wants to do it right.

Don't Be That Girl

Don't get on your phone between every shot. Don't play music unless the group agrees. Don't talk about your divorce on the green (unless you're all crying together, and then—maybe).

Also: don't give unsolicited advice. Even if your friend's swing is all elbows and chaos, or she moves her head all over the place, don't critique it. This isn't a lesson.

But You Do Need Lessons

The best golf lesson I ever received was from Randy Henry—the man who literally patented the process of making custom clubs based on your natural swing. I'm lucky enough to be surrounded by golf wisdom: my son Austin married Randy's daughter Jeni in 2011, so I guess you could say golf is a family affair.

Randy's motto is: "Everyone has a natural swing. Not identical swings." That simple truth changed everything for me. Great golf teachers—like Randy—are worth their weight in gold. He was in a car accident when he was 21. After a year in a cast from breaking 5 vertebrae, he wanted to return to his life as a golf pro. Needless to say, he did not have the same swing. So he invented (and patented) how to determine the proper club for the swing you have. He created a system that helps you build a swing that fits your body, not some cookie-cutter model. The lessons made me stop trying to copy people. Some people have a natural flat, baseball swing. It might not look "perfect' but it's THEIR swing. Some people have really slow, deliberate big swings with great tempo and stop at the top of their backswing. That works for them.

Some pros, unfortunately, try to teach everyone the same way. Generic lessons like "keep your head down! Actually that's a REAL golf rule so listen to that...but someone who tells you to swing as hard as you can probably doesn't have a clue as to REAL golf. Yes, it is clubhead speed that correlates with distance, but it's more the torque of the body than the muscling of the club. And being able to turn a lot is basically dependent on your flexibility (maybe age). It's like going to a shoe store where they only carry size 7 and insisting it'll work for everyone. If you actually wear a size 10, you'll twist and contort just to squeeze in. Sure, you might manage to walk for a while—but eventually, you'll go back to your natural stride. Same with your swing. Your body remembers who it really is. A good teacher doesn't try to shrink you. They help you swing like YOU!

The first thing I learned from Randy is that I had a faster club head swing, so I need a senior men's shaft, not a women's shaft. What in the world! The second issue was that I naturally have a flatter swing, so I need a shaft not in the upright position. So, if you're truly committed to learning this game, get fitted for clubs that fit your natural swing. But you probably should wait for the custom fitting until you figure out what feels natural for you on the course.

Start with the Basics

The second brilliant lesson I received from Randy was to hit 1,000 balls with my feet together. I'm one of those obsessive-compulsive people who, if I'm given a task, I must do it NOW. So I figured if I go to the driving range 10 days in a row and hit 100 balls every day, then I'd give up the game if I didn't get it.

Hitting balls with your feet together builds a great foundation. Especially if you're starting later in life, unlike kids who just naturally swing the club. With your feet together, you'll lose balance if you swing too fast or move your head. You must subtly shift your weight, hold your head still, and hinge your hands.

To this day, if my game starts going amok, I just put my feet back together (I call it "get back into the boat") and it fixes what's really going wrong.

Keep it in Perspective

People who started younger will always have an advantage—they've simply hit more balls. They developed swings that were natural to them. Play YOUR game. Celebrate their success and enjoy your own. If they drive 200 yards and you drive 150, don't worry. You get a stroke; they don't.

Golf is one of the few sports where people of different skill levels and genders can play fairly together. It's all about handicaps and tee placements- more on that later.

But a word of caution—some players inflate their handicaps by only posting bad rounds so they can win net tournaments. Also, beware of psychological games like, "That doesn't look like an 18-handicap swing." Ignore it.

Gems from the Gals

Women say funny things on the course. One woman said "fish" after missed shots—an acronym for 'F* it's still here.' Another elegant lady quipped after we complimented her shot without looking and we told her it sounded great, she looked at where the ball landed in a bad spot and said, 'It's not a "F" symphony.'

I played with a girl the other day who was a fabulous long hitter. She hit a ball off the tee and followed with a disappointed "condom"— we girls asked her to explain— "well it was safe, but it didn't feel good"

Or the old saying a girl said after a shot "that's a son-in- law—It's not what I was looking for but it will do" describing her ball flight.

Mental Game and Rituals

> Best advice I ever received? Don't aim away from trouble. Aim for a target—a tiny spot. Your mind and body can deliver if they're not overloaded.

Girls talk while walking or in the cart, not holding up the game. Once I step onto the tee, I mentally prepare—deep breaths, no more chatter. Just the target.

A book (*Golf's 8 Second Secret* by Mike Bender) studied that the best golfers hit the ball within 8 seconds of putting their tee in the ground. Jack Nicklaus took 10. Most amateurs take longer—and that's often too much thinking.

Let Your Body Lead

Golf is about tempo and confidence—not remembering 18 different swing thoughts. Like walking across a room, your body knows what to do. Trust it. Pick your target. Let your body deliver.

Final Thoughts

So now you're ready to play. Being 'ready' means being out of the cart with a club in hand when it's your turn. Watch others' shots to help find lost balls. Walk fast if you're walking. Approach the green efficiently. Read your putts from the low side.

If you're not willing to practice, maybe golf isn't for you. But if you do commit—focus on your short game. That's where the magic (and lower scores) are.

Golf is a game of honor, respect, and shared experience. The more you learn the little unspoken things, the more fun you—and your friends—will have.

This isn't about perfection. It's about showing up with grace, good humor, and your whole heart. And maybe a spare ball (or three).

Ready to stop nodding politely and actually get the jokes?

Let's speak golf.

Chapter 4: Speaking Golf
Why It Sometimes Feels Like Another Language

"Golf is not about perfection. It's about patience."
-Juli Inkster

By now, you've learned not to stand in someone's putting line and to keep your cart off the greens—but then you step onto a tee box and hear: "Ugh, total duck hook. Should have laid up. At least I've got a CBDO."

Wait, what? Golfers speak in a strange dialect—half tradition, half nonsense, with plenty of sarcasm mixed in. This chapter is your translator. We'll decode the acronyms, slang, and inside jokes so you can laugh along and never feel like an outsider.

By the end, "USGA" will no longer mean United States Golf Association (in real life) but when you hear it on the golf course it means "You Suck Go Again" which will hopefully make you smile internally.

Golf talk sounds serious. Spoiler: Half of it is inside jokes. Let's get you inside.

If you've ever stood on a tee box and wondered what on earth everyone is talking about, you're not alone. Golf has its own dictionary—half tradition, half nonsense, and sometimes just plain funny. Here's your insider's guide to the terms, acronyms, and sayings you'll hear on the course (and a few you'll only hear from girlfriends).

Golf Acronyms (That Aren't in the Rule Book)

Golfers love acronyms—some official, most made up on the fly. These are the ones you'll actually hear out there:

- **USGA** – *You Suck Go Again*
- **CBDO** – *Cry baby Do-Over*
- **FODP** – *Fear of Dark Places* (a ball that looks into the hole and refuses to drop)
- **DF** – *Design Flaw* (aka when a tree is inconveniently in the way)
- **Fish Cost** – F** *It's still here.*
- **Chicken Butt** – *Chip and putt.*
- **GFY** – *Go F** Yourself* (guys say this more than we do).

- **GASP** – *Grip, Alignment, Stance, Posture.*
- **GOLF** – Supposedly "Gentlemen Only, Ladies Forbidden." (Umm… no. Let's redefine it as *Greatest of Life's Frustrations*—or *Go Out, Lose Friends.*)

Tom proofread this book before you, the reader, got to read it...He didn't think it "appropriate' for me to use the "F" word in this book and that's why I replaced it with the word F**…Actually in my REAL world that word floats to the surface of my lips only on the golf course and I feel good when I don't let it escape. It is that IMPOSSIBLE to play this game!

Lingo You'll Hear Everywhere

Some of these are real. Some are jokes. Either way, you'll hear them tossed around like everyone should know what they mean.

- **Birdie** – One under par.
- **Eagle** – Two under par.
- **Albatross** – Three under par. (Rare, but it happens.)
- **Bogey** – One over par.
- **Dormy** – When you can't lose a match.

- **FORE!** – Translation: "Duck, now!"
- **Links** – A specific type of course, mostly in Scotland.
- **PGA** – *Please Go Again.*
- **BOGEY** – *Been Outside Golfing Every Year.*
- **SHOT** – *Should Have Opted for Tennis.*
- **DUFF** – *Didn't Use Full Force.*
- **SAND** – *Some Angry, Nasty Disaster.* (Now there's an image.)

Swing Advice You Didn't Ask For
(But Will Hear Anyway)

Every golfer you meet has their "magic swing key" for you. Some are actually helpful, some...not so much. You'll learn to smile and nod, then keep what works.

- Swing every iron like a wedge.
- Swing down, then around.
- Trust the swing.
- Fire the right side, flat left wrist.
- Soft hands, keep swinging.
- Think: focus—just hit the ball...no one ever hits a ball with their backswing...even if it's perfect

- Head still—don't sway.

- Less is more.

- Clear the hip.

- Knees flex, left heel down for control.

- Don't be handsy.

- No reverse pivot—turn your back to target.

- Keep your left arm straight. (Okay, this one really does work.)

- Lift left heel up on back swing.

- In set up, have weight on inside of back foot.

- Left shoulder up.

- Head behind ball— HOLD HEAD TOTALLY STILL THROUGHOUT SWING.

- Focus on an inch in front of the ball— swing through that spot.

Wisdom from the Pros

Golf may be funny, but it's also timeless. Here are a few favorite quotes that capture its paradox:

"Golf is deceptively simple and endlessly complicated. It satisfies the soul and frustrates the intellectual. A child can play it well and a grown man can never master it. It is almost a science. Yet it is a puzzle without an answer."

— Arnold Palmer

"I know that you believe you understand what you think I said, but I am not sure you heard is not what I meant."

— Robert McCluskey

"Golf is a game whose aim is to hit a very small ball into an even smaller hole with weapons singularly ill-designed for that purpose."

— Winston Churchill

"The most rewarding things you do in life are often the ones that look like they cannot be done."

— **Arnold Palmer**

"I never miss a putt — I just occasionally miss the hole."

— **Gary Player**

"Give me a fast green and a downhill putt and I'll never three-putt...I'll four-putt."

— **Sam Snead**

"If you really want to get better at golf, go back and take it up at a much earlier age."

— **Ben Hogan**

"You can talk to a fade, but a hook won't listen."

— **Lee Trevino**

"Not even God can hit a 1-iron."

— **Lee Trevino**

"Golf is a good walk spoiled."

— Mark Twain

"If you watch a game, it's fun. If you play it, it's recreation. If you work at it, it's golf."

— Bob Hope

CHAPTER 5: Cry Baby Do-Overs
and Other Valid Scoring Methods

"Golf is the most fun you can have without taking your clothes off." -Chi Chi Rodriguez

Keeping score the "official" way when you're brand-new can be demoralizing. Nothing makes a beginner cry faster than stringing together triples, doubles, and lost-ball penalties by the sixth hole. But here's a secret: almost every golfer you know has quietly bent the scoring "rules" just to survive those early rounds.

This chapter isn't about PGA-approved math—it's about staying in the game. You'll learn the beginner-friendly tricks (Cry Baby Do-Overs, Design Flaws, 4L "I'm Lying" notations) that keep scorecards from crushing your spirit. Think of this as training wheels for your golf confidence: a way to track progress, laugh at the inevitable flubs, and—most importantly—want to come back for another round.

Now, I know what you're thinking: *Do we really need a whole chapter on how to keep score?* Yes. Yes, we do. Because if you're just starting out and trying to score "correctly," you're going to cry by the 6th hole—and not just from sun exposure and sand traps. Scoring might be one of the biggest reasons people quit playing at the beginning because it's just adding up TOO MUCH. They think par is the standard number of shots they "should' be hitting to get the ball into the hole. That's too steep of a goal for beginners. It is a GOAL that keeps you swinging, but the truth is unless you're very lucky in the beginning of your golf "career" you won't have very many pars every time you play.

This chapter is not about rules. It's about survival. It's about the secret language of beginner scoring—the "4L"s, the "CBDO"s, and the "DF"s. It's about how to make scoring something that keeps you *playing*, not something that makes you *quit*.

And let's be honest: if you want to feel good about yourself in the beginning, a little creative accounting is practically required.

When I first started, I was not playing with anyone but Tom or some girlfriends who were also beginners. I would come home with a 4L on the card. Tom would say, "What's the L?" I say, "I'm lying. I actually hit it over the green in three, but it was in a spot I couldn't hit from. So, I moved it." "5C" on the scorecard. Tom would say "What's the C mean?" "That means I cheated. I fluffed with this shot and so did the shot again from the same spot. I only hit the ball five times that I counted."

And then Tom would see a 4 on a par 4 but with a CBDO next to it. "What's this?" That's a "cry baby do over." That means I didn't use the first shot because it was a ridiculous flub. Then he saw a "DF." "What's that mean?" "Well, I hit a ball and it hit a tree and it bounced into the water. So, I just called that a Design Flaw because the tree shouldn't have been there."

MY SCORING METHOD

Now that I've become a real golfer, I don't use letters or traditional golf scores on my scorecard anymore. I use small numbers—little mental tricks to keep me going:

−1, 0, 1, 2, 3. That's it. Nothing higher.

Here's what they mean:

- **−1** = birdie (one under par)
- **0** = par
- **1** = bogey (one over par)
- **2** = double bogey
- **3** = triple bogey or worse

That's the cap.

I don't write anything higher than a 3.

This scoring method completely confused Tom.

"Sue, you're reinventing the game," he said.

Maybe so—but mentally, this was the best way for me to stay motivated and actually want to come back out and play. A scorecard filled with 8s? Brutal. Uninspiring. But a card full of 1s, 2s, and a few 0s? *That* I can work with.

What I'm really doing is scoring **against par**, not counting every single swing. Par is the expected number of shots it should take to complete a hole. Most courses have a total par of **72**—usually **36 for the front nine and 36 for the back nine**.

So, here's how my math works.

Let's say on the front nine I write down a **7**. That doesn't mean I shot a 7 on a hole—it means I finished the front nine **seven strokes over par**. Since par for nine holes is 36, I simply add:

36 (par) + 7 (over par) = 43

Then I do the same on the back nine.

If my total for the day is **+7**, I add it to **72**, which gives me a **79**.

Same score.

Much kinder math.

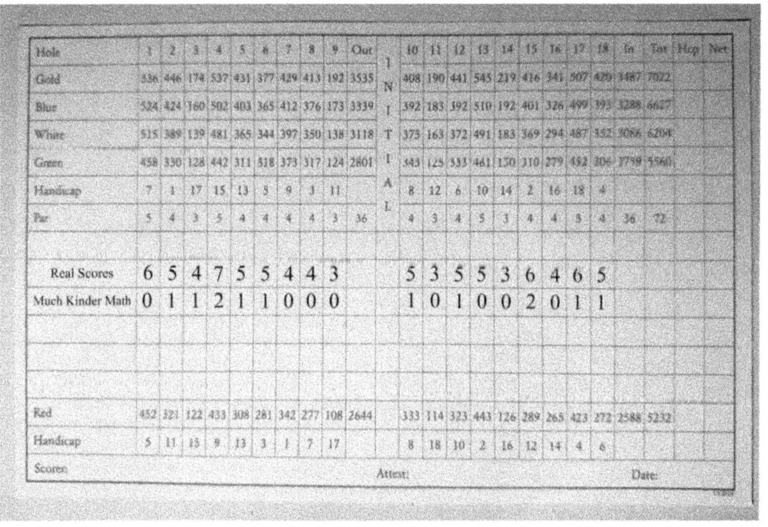

Hole	1	2	3	4	5	6	7	8	9	Out	10	11	12	13	14	15	16	17	18	In	Tot	Hcp	Net
Gold	536	446	174	537	431	377	429	413	192	3535	408	190	441	545	219	416	341	507	429	3487	7022		
Blue	524	424	160	502	403	365	412	376	173	3339	392	183	192	510	192	401	326	499	393	3288	6627		
White	515	389	139	481	365	344	397	350	138	3118	373	163	372	491	183	369	294	487	152	3086	6204		
Green	458	330	128	442	311	318	373	317	124	2801	545	125	333	461	150	310	279	452	306	3759	5560		
Handicap	7	1	17	15	13	5	9	3	11		8	12	6	10	14	2	16	18	4				
Par	5	4	3	5	4	4	4	4	3	36	4	3	4	5	3	4	4	5	4	36	72		
Real Scores	6	5	4	7	5	5	4	4	3		5	3	5	5	3	6	4	6	5				
Much Kinder Math	0	1	1	2	1	1	0	0	0		1	0	1	0	0	2	0	1	1				
Red	452	321	122	433	308	281	342	277	108	2644	333	114	323	443	126	289	265	423	272	2588	5232		
Handicap	5	11	13	9	13	3	1	7	17		8	18	10	2	16	12	14	4	6				
Scores											Attest:											Date:	

The truth is, I want to glance at my card and immediately see how many pars I had—not relive every painful swing and thoughts that weren't effective. This system keeps me focused on patterns, progress, and possibilities...not punishment.

To this day, my friends understand my scoring system. At the end of the round, I'll challenge them to add their scores as fast as I add mine. It usually takes me about ten seconds.

Some of my girlfriends have a tradition when someone makes a birdie. Out comes a tiny celebratory treat—just something sweet that lives in the golf bag for special moments.

I always think a birdie already feels fantastic. Your shoulders drop. Your step gets lighter. You don't really need anything extra...But I'll never say no to a good tradition.

If anything, I've suggested we save the celebratory sip for a triple bogey. *That's* when morale actually needs support.

It's important to understand that golf is a serious game—but if you're just starting out, you *have* to have a sense of humor, or you'll quit before you even give yourself a chance. The truth is, golf can be humbling. That's why I did little things at the beginning to keep it light and make it fun. I still use many of them and if I do say so myself, I'm fun to play with.

For example, I name my golf clubs. My driver is Big Mama. 3-wood? Sweet Baby Girlfriend. The 5-wood is Eduardo. And the 7-wood—Priscilla. I give them names because I want them to feel like friends, not weapons of destruction. It makes me smile when I pull Priscilla out for a shot. We have history.

I also play with yellow golf balls. Not just for visibility—but because I'm a painter, and I *love* yellow. It makes me happy. And that's really what I'm getting at: golf should feel joyful. Sure, it's challenging. But it doesn't have to be stiff or intimidating.

Add your own little rituals. Wear the visor that makes you feel cute. Carry your lucky tee. Dance a little when you finally sink that putt. Whatever keeps you relaxed and smiling—do more of that.

Some gals are very picky about how they take care of their equipment (putting headcovers on after every shot). Others just jam their clubs into the bag with no covers and listen to them clatter against themselves the whole round. That would be me, but I always put my putter head over on to keep it HOT and ready to go. My husband is one who takes care of his clubs and panics if things go awry.

When we were moving all six kids and two dogs from Palm Beach, Florida to North Carolina, we drove two vehicles. Tom was in his Lincoln, pulling a U-Haul trailer. I followed behind in a motor home with four of the kids, my friend since 3rd grade, Connie, and her two kids. We both had nursing babies.

This is how we rolled: a motor home packed with people, random belongings, and a five-gallon Igloo cooler brimming with lemonade.

When I say, "two dogs," I should clarify—one of them was a Great Dane; the other was a blind toy poodle. The Great Dane was not a dog but rather a full grown human with his own seat and digestive surprises. I've always said: little dogs, little problems; big dogs, big problems. And on this particular day, we were about to learn exactly how big.

Somewhere in mid-Georgia, Dr. Bones—the Great Dane—stood up and unleashed explosive diarrhea all over the RV floor.

Pandemonium. Kids screaming. Gagging. Chaos at a whole new Big Dog level.

I pulled over and assessed the scene like a seasoned crisis manager. Step one: kids out of the RV. Step two: the dog. Step three: me, standing by the roadside, realizing we still had eight hours to go—and zero preparation.

No shovel.

No trash bags.

No plan.

Apparently, we'd packed for children, not for gastrointestinal catastrophes of this magnitude.

Desperately scanning the RV, I spotted it: Tom's golf bag. Inside, his prized Pine Valley golf bag cover, name embroidered and all.

Now, I'm a mother of six. Improvisation is my superpower. I didn't hesitate. I unzipped the golf bag cover and used it to clean up the Big Dog disaster. Then I poured lemonade over it to...help things along.

Resourceful?

Absolutely.

Heroic? I'd say yes.

The kids were dramatically gagging on the roadside while I completed the operation. When I finished, I did what any rational person would do: I left the golf cover on the side of the road and got back in the RV.

This was pre–cell phones. There was no group text. No warning. No documentation.

We drove to the next town, where Tom was meeting us. I was hysterical; we all were—laughing and crying—when I told him the entire story.

His eyes were wide with horror.

The first thing out of his mouth:

"You left my Pine Valley golf club cover on the side of I-95 with my name on it?!"

I calmly explained that no one was going to pick up a golf club cover covered in Big Dog problems and read his name. But, just to be fair, I did give him the option to go back and retrieve it.

He did not choose that option.

So somewhere on a road in Georgia, there may still be a Pine Valley golf club cover with Tom Fazio's name on it—marking the site of one unforgettable Big Dog emergency.

GIRLFRIENDS MAKE GOLF MORE FUN

It's fun to play golf with your husband or partner—there's a comfort there, a shared rhythm and something to talk about over dinner. But there's something special, something essential, about playing with other women. Girlfriends bring a whole different kind of energy to the course. There's more laughter, more storytelling, more space to just *be* yourself.

Most of the time, I'm with a girlfriend who's reminiscing about how she used to crush the ball 225 yards, or how she once got out of bunkers like a pro. Then we all start chiming in with our own "back in the day" moments. It's always funny. One of my friends said, "Well, I used to be able to do cartwheels"—and right then and there, on the green, she tried one. The caddies' faces were priceless. They helped peel her off the grass, and we couldn't stop laughing.

I have this friend who told me that her husband wanted her to go get fitted for golf clubs. She thought that they'd measure her, and measure her arms, and maybe measure her shoulders.

She had no idea that she was supposed to hit 100 balls in front of this pro while he took pictures. Talk about intimidating for a beginner golfer.

So those clubs she got were certainly clubs that fit the golfer that she was at that moment in her life. But now that she's developed a swing, they may not fit so much anymore. And now that she's not so intimidated by having someone watch her hit the balls.

See, men just don't understand. They don't understand the performance anxiety women go through when they are trying to hit a golf ball in front of a stranger. I don't know why, but I feel it myself all the time. It's like we feel they're judging us. Against all the great golfers they know.

The truth is, it is kind of like going to a gynecologist and being nervous and humble about opening your legs. He's seen a lot of these before. But it still doesn't keep us from being embarrassed.

So back to golf...that kind of fun, that kind of freedom? It's what makes the game magical. Now, you're definitely not supposed to be doing cartwheels on a golf course- but hey, we were beginners. We cheer for each other, we console each other, and we don't take ourselves too seriously—unless it's about snacks after the 18th hole.

The first time I played in a tournament was with three women who were just as new and nervous as I was. We won AND we had the best time. It was at Calcutta and there was a lot of money for the winners. They had given our group 36 shots, and I knew with that many shots we could win.

We got to the 17th tee, and my one friend's husband was standing on the par three green waiting for us to tee off. His wife wouldn't swing if he was watching, but he wouldn't budge. So, I suggested if we all mooned him, he would leave. So we did and he left. We get to the green, and my husband is standing there with a real concern on his face. He says, "He just told me you all mooned him." I told him why. He said very seriously, "Sue, there's a lot of people on the 18th green. It won't be good if you moon them." "Good thing we were on 17!" My foursome won the money and laughed all the way home.

When I took up golf when I was 60, I was told golf was a good way to make friends. I thought I had more than enough friends. What golf has done for me is create real quality time to develop real relationships with wonderful women. There is no such thing as having too many friends.

Cry Baby Do-Overs and creative scoring keep you laughing long enough to stay in the game. But once you're hooked, you'll realize: etiquette sets the tone—next comes the respect, rhythm, and rules that make people actually want to play with you again.

CHAPTER 6: Respect, Rhythm, and the Rules
Don't make your bad day ruin everyone else's day.
Etiquette for People Who Still Want Friends
After 18 Holes

"The Most Important thing in golf is attitude."

-Nancy Lopez

The Heart of Golf Etiquette

Golf is a civilized game. It's built on respect—for your partners, for the course, for the rules, and for yourself. Etiquette is everything:

- No slapping your club on the ground if you've hit a bad shot—it's not the ground's fault.
- Don't wear spikes and grind your foot into the ground—it leaves a mark.
- Rake your trap and leave it like it was before.
- If you see trash/ pick it up!

- If you see a divot that's like a huge dunk of grass/ dirt (even if you didn't make it), replace it.
- Keep your cool after a shanked drive or a totally terrible shot.
- Keep your volume low.
- Keep the vibe enjoyable.

It's not about being perfect—it's about creating an experience that people actually want to be part of. No one enjoys 18 holes with a sulker, a club-slammer, or someone screaming at the clouds (even if the wind did sabotage your shot). No one enjoys playing with a mean-spirited, self-absorbed woman either. Self-awareness is the real secret sauce.

A decent attitude, a playlist at the right volume (or just in your head), and knowing when to offer help—or when to just say, "tough break"—can change the entire round.

Knowledge Is Confidence

Nothing builds confidence on the course like knowing the rules. Not so you can be *that person* who corrects everyone else (please, don't), but so you can stand tall in your own game. Integrity in golf isn't about perfection—it's about awareness. When you know the rules, you can protect your score, your playing partners, and the flow of the round.

Take one example: you're only allowed three minutes to search for a lost ball. That's not a suggestion—it's the rule. Hanging around in the rough for 10 minutes while the groups behind you stack up isn't just annoying—it throws off the rhythm of the entire course.

And while golf has long been called a "gentleman's game," that phrase feels outdated. Golf is for honest, respectful humans lucky enough to play it—women, men, kids, beginners, pros, everyone. Respect isn't gendered, it's universal.

Following the rules is less about rigidity and more about showing care for the people you're playing with and the game itself.

The more you learn the rules, the freer you feel. You stop second-guessing yourself; you stop worrying if you're "doing it right," and you gain the quiet confidence of someone who knows they belong on the course. That kind of self-assurance is magnetic—and it makes the game a whole lot more fun.

Learn from the Pros (But Stay Human)

Want to know what a calm, composed presence looks like? Watch the pros. They're not just hitting balls—they're managing energy, nerves, and focus. Their head stays still. Their left arm stays straight through the backswing. Their breathing is deliberate: inhale for 4, exhale for 6. Pro tip: breathing isn't just oxygen—it's golf's built-in meditation. Relax. Wiggle your toes. Rock gently back and forth. Heck, dance a little over the ball if that calms your nerves. The calmer your body, the clearer your focus.

You can see the peace in a pro.

The Women's Advantage

Women bring something powerful to this game: perspective. We don't usually throw tantrums when we play badly. We don't scream at the wind. We accept it and move on. Maybe it's because life has trained us: the feverish child, the urgent work call, the maintenance guy who shows up two hours late. We roll with it. And in that way, women were made for this game.

Tips from the Pros (and from Life)

- Keep your head still. Think "steady tripod."
- Straight left arm creates consistency in your swing.
- Breathe. Inhale for 4, exhale for 6. Calm body = clear focus.
- Know the rules. Knowledge is power. (Three minutes to find a ball. Period.)
- Respect the game. Lower the music, mind your temper, and keep the play moving.
- Stay playful. Dance over the ball if you need to—it's your game.
- Listen to a song in your mind if it helps—but don't hum it aloud unless everyone's into it.

You've got the courtesies down, and your foursome still likes you—good. Etiquette sets the tone—next comes the mental game that keeps you smiling through the shanks, handling the hazards, and trusting yourself when everything feels wobbly.

Having a pre-shot routine is critical to building confidence…your pre-shot routine can be anything that gets you ready to hit the ball. However, it should be considerate of other golfers' time. If the acceptable pre-shot routine is 8-10 seconds, according to Mike Benders' *Golf's 8 Second Secret,* then a gal who takes 25 seconds is using up other golfers' time. Sometimes it's a deliberate attempt to rattle her opponents. But pre-shot routines are essential for all good golfers.

Tom and I were playing golf with Nick and Sue Price and since he's considered one of the fastest PGA players I asked him about what I should do if someone seems like they are deliberately slowing down to make their opponents get aggravated. He told me that when he was playing with a slow player, rather than walk faster he slowed his pace down.

CHAPTER 7: Fear — Why the Biggest Hazard is in Your Head

"Thinking instead of acting is the number one golf disease." -Sam Snead

Golf will expose you.

Not just your slice or your short game—but your brain. The overthinking, the nerves, the sudden panic when everyone's watching, and you realize you have no idea how you're supposed to pull this off. Sound familiar?

Don't worry—you're not broken. You're human.

Golf asks for focus but punishes overthinking. The line between the two is razor thin and learning how to walk it is the difference between enjoying the round and wanting to throw your club into the nearest pond. This chapter isn't about fixing your swing. It's about quieting your mind.

The Yips and Performance Anxiety

Bob Rotella, world-renowned sports psychologist, says there's no such thing as the yips (a sudden, involuntary loss of fine motor control in experienced athletes)—it's just fear masquerading as failure.

FEAR: False Events Appearing Real.

That fear can show up anywhere: on the tee, in the bunker, over a short putt. And for many women, it's especially loud—not because we're weaker, but because we care.

Rotella's entire philosophy boils down to this: practice and learn off the course—but once you're playing, get out of your own way. No fixing. No thinking. No commentary. Let the body perform what it already knows.

The problem is, fear doesn't let us do that.

That feeling usually starts long before golf. Somewhere in childhood, you tried something new, failed, and someone laughed. That moment got stored in the emotional "bank." Years later, when you're standing over a shot you haven't mastered, that old memory gets withdrawn—with interest.

I've felt it more times than I can count.

I remember standing on a tee box one morning, nervous before I even put the ball on the tee. My heart was racing. And my thoughts were already spiraling:

Don't hit it left. Don't top it. Don't embarrass yourself.

Here's the thing I've learned—on the course and in life: you have to focus on what you *want* to happen, not what you don't.

The minute your thoughts start with the word *don't*—Don't hit it in the water. Don't top it. Don't embarrass yourself — fear has taken the steering wheel.

Your body doesn't hear the *don't*. It only hears *water, top, embarrass*—and then, obediently, it tries to deliver exactly that.

Years ago, I took a class called *Mastery of Words*, where I learned something called the emotional tone scale. I didn't realize then that it would perfectly apply to golf—but it does.

At the top of the scale are the words of confidence and freedom:

I am. I can. I will.

That's where Rotella wants you playing from. Calm. Present. Trusting.

But the moment something hurts—emotionally or physically—the first response is often:

Ouch.

If you don't catch it there, the spiral begins.

Next comes anger: He moved. She talked. The wind did this. This course is ridiculous.

If that doesn't resolve, it drops into grief: Poor me. Why does this always happen to me? That heavy, embarrassed feeling that follows you to the next hole like a bad smell.

From there, it sinks into apathy: I can't. And if you stay there long enough: I don't want to. I won't.

That's when people quit—not just the round, but the game.

Here's the good news—and this is where Rotella and the emotional scale meet: you don't have to climb the whole ladder back up.

If you hit a terrible shot—and you will—the practice is simple:

Don't blame it. Don't explain it. Don't carry it.

That shot is over.

Name what you *do* want:

Smooth. Pause. Target.

Rotella says the best players commit fully to the next shot and leave the last one behind. Golf just makes the emotional feedback faster and louder. You can feel when you're rising—or falling.

So, when you hear *don't* in your head, treat it like a warning light on the dashboard.

Fear is driving.

Gently take the wheel back—and aim where you actually want to go.

So back to my shot. Of course, I rushed. Of course, I didn't breathe. And of course, the ball went exactly where I didn't want it to go.

The worst part wasn't the shot—it was the feeling afterward. That hot wave of self-criticism. That voice saying, *"You should be better than this."*

I've felt it in my body, too. My left thumb shakes on short shots. I fear missing something I "should" make. I used to rush just to get it over with—anything to escape that feeling.

Now, when my thumb shakes, I count:

1, 2, 3, 4. I give my brain a stronger job than fear.

One Thought is Plenty

Here's another piece of great advice I've been given. "If you're thinking, you're stinking."

Do your thinking on the practice range. On the course, choose one thought. Just one.

Mine is: pause.

Slow back. Stop at the top. Swing through.

When I'm walking up to the ball, I might remind myself of posture or follow-through. But once I address it, it's just: *pause*.

One word quiets the noise.

And a quiet mind lets the body do what it already knows how to do.

Missing is Not Failure

Every shot is some combination of distance and direction. And guess what? Even professionals miss. A lot.

The average PGA tour player makes a six-foot putt 70% of the time. Let that sink in. If the best in the world don't expect perfection, why should you?

Golf is not a referendum on your worth.

It's a series of attempts.

Fear on the course is rarely about the shot in front of you. It's about the shot behind you. It's about an old memory, an old judgment, an old voice saying, *"Don't mess this up."* Play with a good golfer. It's amazing. They get into trouble and use a great amazing shot to get back into play. The beginner golfer is in there, thick into self-loathing and embarrassment, and swings fast so she can get it over with!

The skill is learning how to replace that voice. Breathe. Count. Repeat your word.

You don't eliminate fear—you outfocus it.

And here's something else I wish I had known earlier: most people aren't watching nearly as closely as you think. They're worrying about their own shot, their own swing, and their own score. The spotlight you feel is usually one you're shining on yourself.

Final Word on Fear

The biggest hazards in golf aren't water or sand.

They're rushing. They're spiraling. They're taking themselves too seriously.

Golf rewards presence. It rewards preparation. And it always rewards patience. Calm your mind first.

CHAPTER 8: From Tee Box to Green:
What the Range Doesn't Teach You

"The most important shot in golf is the next one."
-Ben Hogan

The driving range is polite. It's flat, predictable, and forgiving. The mat doesn't judge you; the ball sits up nicely every time, and no one is watching you decide which club to pull while your heart pounds. The golf course, on the other hand, has opinions. It introduces wind, slopes, uneven lies, and an audience—sometimes all at once. This chapter is about what happens when practice ends, and real golf begins.

One of the first things you notice on the course is that no two lies are the same. At the range, every shot feels fair. On the course, the ground tilts, the ball settles awkwardly, and suddenly you're not sure how to stand. And you're basically chasing after your ball, driving your cart around looking for it only to find it on the left of the fairway behind a tree.

An uphill lie adds loft, so the ball goes higher and shorter—play it forward in your stance, take more club, keep shoulders parallel to slope.

-SIDE BAR-

When golfers say "take more club," they don't mean swing harder. They mean choose a longer club than you normally would for that distance.

For example:

- If you would usually hit a 7-iron from that distance,
- you'd "take more club" and use a 6-iron instead.

Why?

An uphill lie adds loft, which makes the ball fly higher but shorter. So even though the distance *looks* the same, the ball won't travel as far.

A downhill lie does the opposite; play the ball back, take less club, and match your shoulders to the slope. Sidehill lies have their own personality. When the ball is above your feet, it wants to go left—use less loft and aim right. When it's below your feet, it wants to leak right—

use more loft and aim left. These aren't mistakes; they're physics. Once you accept that, the course feels less hostile and more honest.

The tee box is another place the range doesn't prepare you for. Wind matters here—more than you think. Into a headwind, tee it lower. With a tailwind, tee it higher. If your natural ball flight moves right to left, tee the ball on the right side of the box, and vice versa. These are small adjustments, but they add up. Golf is rarely about big fixes; it's about stacking smart choices.

And then there's the mental shift. On the range, you can hit ten bad shots in a row and no one cares. On the course, one bad shot can feel like a public announcement of incompetence. This is where fear sneaks in. The truth is, the biggest hazards aren't water or sand—they're in your head. Thinking too much, rushing, or trying to "fix" something mid-round almost always makes things worse. The range is for thinking. The course is for trusting.

Practice, too, looks different once you understand how the game is actually scored. Everyone loves hitting the driver, but you'll use it at most fourteen times a round. Putts? About half your score. Chips and pitches? Constantly. Spending an hour pounding drivers might feel productive but spending that time learning how to get the ball close from around the green will lower your score faster than any new club ever could. That's not glamorous advice—but it's true.

Short game is where confidence is built quietly. Learning how far your wedges go with different swing lengths—seven o'clock, eight o'clock, nine o'clock— gives you control. Writing those distances down turns guessing into knowing. Once you stop just trying to get the ball "on the green" and start trying to get it close, golf feels less random and more intentional.

Bunkers deserve their own paragraph because they carry so much unnecessary shame. Most people don't hate sand traps; they hate the memory of failing in them. One good lesson from a pro—not your husband—can change everything. Learn one simple technique, practice it enough to feel competent, and then stop replaying old disasters. Even professionals don't get out every time. Sand is not a moral failing. The architect designed it to 'protect' the green. That's what my husband tells me. I tell him, "Who's protecting ME? That green doesn't need protecting—I do!"

The course also teaches you how to move. Pace matters. Being ready, choosing your club while others hit, walking with purpose—these things keep the round enjoyable for everyone, including you. Golf doesn't require rushing your swing; it requires being prepared. There's a difference.

By the time you reach the green, you realize something important: real golf isn't about perfect shots. It's about recovery, adjustment, and acceptance. The course will never look like the range, and that's the point. It asks you to think less, feel more, and trust what you've practiced.

What the range doesn't teach you is how to be with yourself when things go sideways. The course does. It teaches patience, humility, and resilience—one uneven lie at a time.

And once you understand that, the game becomes less intimidating and far more generous.

- **Uphill lie**

  The ball goes higher and shorter.

  Play it forward. Take more club.

- **Downhill lie**

  The ball comes out lower and runs.

  Play it back. Take less club.

  Keep shoulders parallel to the slope.

- **Ball above your feet**

  Tends to hook left.

  Use less loft. Aim right.

  AR = Aim Right

- **Ball below your feet**

  Tends to slice right.

  Use more loft. Aim left.

  AL = Aim Left

  Simple. Logical. Learnable.

Tee Box Tricks

A few things every woman should know:

- Tee it **low** into a headwind
- Tee it **high** into a tailwind
- If your ball curves right-to-left, tee up on the **right** side of the box (and vice versa)
- When in doubt, do the opposite of your instinct— it's usually closer to correct

Practice vs. Power

Ben Hogan said it best: "The will to succeed is important, but the will to prepare is even more important."

Another 20 yards off the tee doesn't matter as much as an 8-foot chip instead of a 20-footer.

If you have an hour to practice: (this is only opinion)

- 15 minutes: full swings
- 45 minutes: chipping and pitching

Drivers are used maybe 14 times a round.

Short game? Constantly.

Creative Chipping for Real Results

Stop aiming just to get it on the green. Aim to get it **close**.

Learn your distances:

- Pick your wedges (60°, 56°, 50°, PW)
- Practice backswings stopping at 7, 8, and 9 o'clock
- Write down how far the ball flies and rolls

This knowledge saves strokes fast.

Tracking Your Game (Without Judgment)

I track four things:

- **D** = Drives
- **F** = Fairways
- **C** = Chips
- **P** = Pitches/Approach shots

Mark each as great, average, or poor.

Patterns tell the truth—not emotion.

Bunker Battles

Most golfers don't hate bunkers. They hate the *memory* of failing in them.

Visualization works better than embarrassment.

Hazards and Common Mistakes

- **Yellow stakes:** drop where it entered
- **White stakes:** replay from original spot
- **Red stakes:** hit or drop with penalty
- **Reverse pivot:** if you finish on your back foot, fix it by holding your finish—hips to target

Final Word on Playing the Course

Knowing what to do quiets fear and preparation creates confidence. Confidence creates calm and calm makes golf fun again. You don't need to play perfectly; you just need to keep moving forward. Mind settled, tools in hand. Let's play.

CHAPTER 9: The Quiet Hero: Why Putting Wins Rounds

"I'm about touch and feel.
That's what putting is all about."
-Ben Crenshaw

Nearly half of your strokes happen on the green. Think about that: you can crush a 230-yard drive, crisply hit a 7-iron, and still wreck your scorecard with a three-putt. The flat stick quietly decides everything—making putting not a side skill, but *the* skill. That's why this chapter matters: master a little here, and you'll save more strokes than any new driver ever could.

Why the Flat Stick Matters

If golf were a movie, the putter would be the quiet hero—the character everyone underestimates until the last act, the one who saves the day. Drivers get the applause, chips look heroic, but putting? Putting decides everything. Nearly half of your strokes happen on the green.

This chapter is your permission slip to take putting seriously—without taking yourself too seriously. It's where rhythm, touch, and mindset come together. Mastering putting isn't about perfection—it's about presence, patience, and playfulness.

Honor Your Process (and Guard it Fiercely)

Putting is part skill, part rhythm, and part confidence. Create your own ritual—and protect it. Maybe you take a deep breath, visualize the line, or tap the putter twice. Whatever it is, keep it consistent and keep it quick. Watch the pros: every one of them has a pre-shot routine they repeat every single time. They don't second-guess it, and they certainly don't let anyone interrupt it.

Speaking of putting—it is deeply personal. And yet, everyone wants to tell you how to do it. How many new lady golfers step up to line their putt only to have their husband immediately chime in? If you miss, he'll say, "You moved," or "You changed something." If you make it? Suddenly, it was his tip that made it happen. Sound familiar?

Here's the truth: there is no single "right" way to putt. Watch enough tournaments and you'll see every grip, stance, and style imaginable. The only universal is a repeatable ritual. And remember that first-lesson overload—head down, belly button to the hole, relax, butt out, shoulder back...? Don't import that chaos onto the green. Filter it to one simple thought.

Mine: "smooth tempo." I actually love to putt…not because I'm a good putter but because it is a learnable skill. You might not be able to perfect that pivot with your hips or start the follow-through with your leading hip, but there's nothing in your age or history that stops you from being a good putter.

The Green is a Temple (Etiquette that Settles Nerves)

Treat the putting surface like sacred ground:

- Walk lightly, never step on another player's line (the invisible path between their ball and the hole).
- Be still when someone is over the ball—movement in their peripheral vision can throw them off.
- If you're first to finish, tend or replace the flagstick.

This quiet respect doesn't just help others—it settles your own nerves.

Reading the Putts: Distance Before Direction

Everyone has advice. You'll see players crouching behind their ball, pacing circles like detectives. My husband's favorite tip? "Imagine dumping a bucket of water on the green—that's where your ball will roll." My response: "I don't carry a bucket of water."

Here's the designer's secret: greens are built to drain in one or two directions. Course architects can "see" that instantly; the rest of us learn by trial and error.

Numbers Tell the Story:

PGA Tour Pros typically average only about 77 % from 5 feet, 40 % from 10 feet, and 88 % overall inside 10 feet.

That means roughly:

- 8 out of 10 five-foot putts go in
- 2 out of 10 are missed-even by the best players in the world

For a little perspective: Typical make percentages by distance on the PGA Tour are approximately:

Distance	Make %
3 feet	~99%
4 fcct	~90-92%
5 feet	~80%
6 feet	~70%
10 feet	~40%

If the best in the world can't sink everything, why should you expect to? Often, it isn't your stroke, but your read that betrays you—misjudge slope, break, or speed and par turns into bogey.

When you miss, reset, breathe, and move on. If the pros can lip out a five-footer and still win, you can miss a few and still have a great round.

Systems That Build Confidence

There are methods to crack green-reading, and the one that changed everything for me was **AimPoint**. Before AimPoint, I was guessing—imaginary buckets of water sloshing in my head. After AimPoint, I had a method. Too detailed to unpack here, but AimPoint seminars are everywhere, and they're worth every penny if you want reliable reads.

Drills That Make Distance Second Nature

Putting is a blend of distance and direction—but distance matters more. Two favorite drills:

- **Toe-to-Toe Speed Check:** Find a level hole. Take your stance and stroke three putts moving the putter from your right foot to your left foot—same length, smooth tempo. Step off that distance (toe-to-toe). That's your baseline. Use it on course and adjust for slope.

- **Ladder Drill (8 Feet and In):** The ladder drill means that you put tees at 10'/8'/6'/ 4'/2' around a hole...put 10 balls in a circle around that hole at each footage— that's 50 balls— Practice! Practice! Practice! (Actually, you're starting on the 2'circle first. And when you can sink all of those— move back to 4'...etc...that will build skill and confidence.

Personal & Quirky Tips That Stick

The basics are the same for everyone: head still, find your line or spot, then release. But quirks are personal:

- A friend told me, "Hold your head over the ball. If you have a runny nose, the snot would hit the ball." You'll never forget that visual.
- Another taught me a cadence for putts 8 feet and under:
    1. Look at the hole.
    2. Look at the ball.
    3. Pull the putter back slowly.
    4. Release. Counting leaves no room for overthinking—it's just rhythm.

If fear creeps in, remember FEAR = False Events Appearing Real. Replace it with a stronger signal: count to four, breathe 4-in/6-out, or repeat your single word ("smooth," "roll," or mine: "pause").

Guard Your Routine Against Interruption

If someone starts coaching you mid-putt? Smile, step away, reset, and start again. Your process is yours. Guard it like a secret recipe.

Laughter on the Green

Laughter resets your body better than any tip. I remember one round where I was completely in my head. I'd missed two short putts in a row; my shoulders were up around my ears, and I was doing that thing where you pretend you're fine, but you're actually spiraling. As I'm standing there trying not to rush my next putt, one of my girlfriends casually says, "Well… at least your outfit is still winning." She wasn't wrong. I laughed, relaxed, and made the putt, finally.

Simply having the mental image of something off the golf course that makes your feeling of calmness open up is helpful. Mine is laying on a raft in a swimming pool with the sun shining brightly and a small breeze. I think of that when I'm playing and my whole body relaxes.

Final Word on the Flat Stick

Putting isn't about perfection—it's about presence. It's the storyteller of your round: every roll writes a line you'll remember long after you walk off the green. Guard your ritual, trust your read, keep it playful, and remember—when the ball lips out, the story isn't over. It's just another plot twist on the path to your next great putt.

Chapter 10: Final Thoughts from the 19th Hole
Why We Keep Coming Back

"Golf is the closest game to the game we call life." -
Bobby Jones

My husband taught me everything HE knows about golf— but not everything I know.

I just returned from a golf trip to Ireland/Scotland. I played Adare/ Ballybunion/ Portrush/ Royal Countydown/ St. Andrews/ Jubilee/ Kingsbarnes with Kalos Travel Company. Fifteen of our friends came and we had a lot of fun! So, see? Golf will take you to special places with great friends that without golf you'd never get like the whole Irish/ Scottish experience. For such a trip you MUST bring rain gear!!! And you simply cannot play without caddies. I normally prefer to play without caddies because I do not like to feel observed, and as I know most caddies are scratch or single digit handicappers and I feel so stupid hitting bad shots in front of them. However, when I was in Ireland, I learned a critical lesson for me...about MY game.

My caddies never told me what to do other than show me what my target was and then after the shot were so complimentary. "Perfect" "great shot" "amazing"— now obviously all of my shots were not perfect, great or amazing BUT the caddies made me feel that way. They never said what my husband often says... "You moved your head/ you swayed/ you swung too fast/ you didn't pause in your backswing..." and I did play really well. But now, after evaluating the games, I believe I played well because my caddies only said positive things to me. I only hit poor shots when I got distracted from my ONE SWING thought (pause in back swing). If someone was talking or I had a thought like (this is teed too low or I think I've got the wrong club) and swung anyway…so my lesson was: I play better when the "coach" is not correcting my swing on the course.

An invaluable lesson I hope my husband learned from me because Tom really wants me to play well. You should practice at the driving range but play with the game you brought! Leave your coach at the practice range.

Decide which ONE swing 'thought' you are going to use when you're on the course and stick with that. Unclutter your mind. Enjoy your game for what it is!

Now that you've "mastered" the practice routines you may think you are ready to play golf well...that thought most certainly calls the GOLF GOD down to earth to do an "attitude adjustment." You must somehow merge cocky with humble.

I was playing in a Member-Guest at Emerald Dunes, and I could do no wrong— shot a 79! The next day, I went to Seminole for a Member-Guest and shot a 113!!! But most of that I blamed on the caddie. I hit my drive on the first hole, and it was in the middle of the fairway. I'm not a long driver but mostly I'm accurate. I asked my caddie for my 3-wood, and he flat out wouldn't give it to me 'women should not have 3-woods in their bags'. Now I had just played my best round the day before, and I used that 3-wood a bunch with good results. But I have a humble streak that surfaces on the golf course, and I'll let someone who has more history in golf take over my game. After that remark and attitude, I sliced (unintentionally) a 7-wood shot into the lake. It was downhill all the way after that. One remark by someone I respected crashed the winning wave I was on.

You leave pieces of yourself on the golf course every time you play. Make sure they are SHINY and JOYOUS pieces—the grass has enough fertilizer already. I always think I'll have a hole-in-one when I stand up to a par three (I've had two so far). That belief is not without its difficulties, but it's better to think that than to remember the last time you stood up and hit your ball in the water.

I used to be quite psychic which means I could tell people's fortunes/knew their illnesses. That cycle for me has passed and now I try to focus that ability onto where the ball is going to go—it's not translated into anything predictable—you've got to take yourself lightly if you're going to take golf seriously.

I have plaques all over my house that have been given to me by my children or well-meaning friends. So I read them constantly and it helps keep things in perspective:

-MY OPINIONS MAY HAVE CHANGED, BUT NOT THE FACT THAT I'M RIGHT!!

-I DONT SUFFER FROM INSANITY…I ENJOY EVERY MINUTE OF IT.

-YOU CALL IT CHAOS…WE CALL IT FAMILY!

-NOTICE—DUE TO THE CURRENT WORKLOAD, THE LIGHT AT THE END OF THE TUNNEL HAS BEEN SWITCHED OFF.

-MIRROR, MIRROR ON THE WALL –WHAT THE @&*^%#@$!! HAPPENED?

-I WILL ALWAYS STRIVE TO BE THE PERSON MY DOG THINKS I AM.

-WHEN A WOMAN SAYS "WHAT?" ITS NOT BECAUSE SHE DIDN'T HEAR YOU, SHE'S JUST GIVING YOU THE CHANCE TO CHANGE WHAT YOU HAVE SAID.

-WE MUST TAKE ADVENTURES TO KNOW WHERE WE TRULY BELONG.

-SOMETIMES IN LIFE…IT JUST IS WHAT IT IS…

-GREAT WOMEN RAISE GREAT WOMEN WHO RAISE GREAT WOMEN.

-LET ME DROP EVERYTHING AND WORK ON YOUR PROBLEM.

I have many more but these sort of help me get REAL when I start thinking I really know anything about ANYTHING so please take these words as mere twinkles of sunlight in the great fog that surrounds us when we are learning anything new...and HARD!

We come to the course for the golf, but we stay for everything else: the friendships, the laughter, the stories that live on long after the scorecard is in the trash. We stay for the challenge that never ends, for the tiny victories that keep us hooked, for the way one pure swing can erase three holes of chaos and make us fall in love all over again. This is like motherhood to me. The frustration of a child who spills a cup of cocoa on a white sofa dissolves when she looks up at you and says, "I'm sorry."

At the end of the day, golf is not really about the numbers. It's about the walk. It's about the sunshine, the breeze, and the girlfriend who has you laughing so hard on the 7th fairway you nearly wet your golf skirt. It's about learning patience when your ball finds yet another bunker—and discovering that you can do hard things, sometimes badly at first, but better the next time.

Golf is a mirror. It shows you where you rush, where you freeze, where you doubt yourself—and then it teaches you how to breathe, how to focus, how to let go. The game strips away the noise: no excuses, no shortcuts, just you, the club, and the ball. And then, like grace, it builds you back up—one steady breath, one good decision, one honest shot at a time.

The game has taught me so much about myself. If someone asked me what the single most important life lesson there is to learn, I'd have to say PATIENCE! Being a mother of six children certainly prepared me for backing into patience when my natural sense of myself is doing it fast/ get it over with. Pottery demands patience and focus. Skiing requires being patient while letting the turn reach its peak before shifting weight to the other edge. Going to a doctor's office. Waiting for repairmen who give you a time and then overshoot that time by 3 hours. Doing an underpainting for a painting requires patience to let it dry before you begin the next level. Waiting for a plane that has been delayed. I could go on and on about the triggers to my impatience. But every shot on the golf course demands patience.

Focus is hard to sustain if you're feeling emotional about your bad playing. Create a trigger when you are feeling less than positive about yourself. Make it your own. I look up into the sky and focus on a cloud shape that's interesting...anything that you can do that will release you from spiraling into despair.

The truth is, golf will expose you. The shaky thumb, the overthinking brain, the bunker that makes you want to cry—yes, they'll all show up. But so will your grit. So will your humor. So will your girlfriends. Around carts, across fairways, and over a glass at the 19th hole, the game will connect you—to yourself, to each other, and sometimes even to your husband (on a good day).

I play in a Saturday game with a group of friends and bet $5. It's not about winning or losing; it's about showing up and trying. It's about being part of a team. The leader of that game shoots out a recap afterwards on an email that is always hilarious and a reason to keep coming back even if you didn't have one of the seven birdies that day.

This game gives a thousand tiny do-overs disguised as shots. It humbles you, it frustrates you, and then it hands you a moment of magic that keeps you coming back. That's the real win. Not the perfect round, but the persistent one. Not the flawless swing, but the fearless one. Not the trophy, but the togetherness.

I think good golfers' brains are probably like golf balls, not any crevices, just a lot of dimples.

I would give up golf some days but then I think "what am I going to do with all of these golf clothes" ...and I continue...

So, keep playing. Keep laughing. Keep showing up with grace, grit, and girlfriends. Play fast, be kind, fix your divots, and forgive your misses. Aim for a tiny spot, breathe like a pro, and remember: the biggest hazard isn't sand or water—it's in your head. Fortunately, you've learned what to do with that.

In the end, whether you shoot a 72 or a 102, what matters most is that you played. You walked. You tried. You cheered. You were there—for the game, for your people, and for yourself. Carry that off the course and into the rest of your life, and you've already won. **Play on.**

LAST MINUTE NOTES FROM
MY PRO—MORGAN

Putting:

- When walking up to the green, walk around the hole and look at the putt from behind the flag, find initial thoughts of how the green reads, then walk to your ball and look at it from there.
- Take practice swing, walk behind the ball to find alignment, than walk into set up.

Short Game: When hitting a bump and run shot, use a pitching wedge or hybrid. (Hybrid will roll more).

-With a pitching wedge

- Narrow stance, put ball back in stance, stand taller, pressure left
- Choose where you want the ball to hit and judge backswing length accordingly (a good way to practice may be to associate backswing length with ankle high, shin high, etc.)

-Using a hybrid

- Same set up as the pitching wedge
- Putt with the hybrid

Full Swing: You liked the idea of looking at or in front of the ball.

Pre-swing process—Practice swing first, then step behind the ball to find the intermediate target in the ground to line up to, step into the ball with the clubface lining up with your chosen intermediate target.

- Grip the club more in the fingers of your hands. Left hand will be more "on top" of the club with the "V" made between your thumb and pointer finger towards your right shoulder.
- With Driver—Ball inside of left heel, pressure 50%/50% in feet. Slight pause at the top, then hit!

- 5 wood—Ball position is one ball behind driver, 55%-60% pressure on left foot.
  - o If contact gets squirrely and you start hitting the ball low or topping it, try to keep the arms extended at the ball and through the ball.

    i.e. We put a tee in front of the ball on the driving range and I had you try to hit the ball then the tee to keep the club lower through the ball longer.

- Hybrid/7 iron—same idea as 5 wood

Bunker:

- Ball position forward similar to a driver, pressure 60%-70% left.
- Hit the sand directly behind the ball, finish facing the target with body and club.

<u>Sue Fazio Lesson Notes 4/4/26</u>

Full swing:

- Tilt shoulders more to the right with the Driver for loft and better movement
- We like a little left hip bump over left shoe and right shoulder tilt with all clubs

Short Game:

Bunker:

- Ball position inside left shoe
- Pressure 70%-80% left
- Hinge wrists in the backswing and use the core to drive through to the target!

Chipping (Low shot with pitching wedge):

- Narrow stance (two clubheads apart)
- Ball inside right foot (right foot roll)
- Feeling closer and taller

- Chest tilts over left shoe! (Opposite of full swing!) This helps keep your center and pressure 60% on left side while chipping.

- Finish with buttons and belt buckle towards target (The arms can't do it alone!)

Putting:

Pace Control-

- Experimenting with left hand low

-Feel the left hand push the putter back and then let the putter fall into the ball instead of "hitting" it to make it get to the hole.

-For you it felt like there was no power in the stroke. Let the putter do the work!

Green reading:

- Continuing to look at the read from behind the ball, then walk around the hole to see if the perspective is different than before.

- Continue to use what you feel under your feet as a guide!

Drill:

Put two tees about 3 feet behind the hole and see if you can get the ball to stop between the flag and the tees. This way if you hit it in your zone, you feel comfortable making the next putt!

Epilogue

So hopefully you have finished this book with a joy and promise that there's nothing to be afraid of on the golf course...even as a beginner. Golf has given me so many hours of joy and laughter. But there's one thing I didn't even get into in this book, but it is worth noting.

I had three whiplash accidents in my early twenties…two in cars that I was driving /stopped at a stop sign and plowed into by someone behind and the last one while I was in the woods meditating. A squirrel jumped next to me/ I jerked my head and ruptured a disc in my neck. Ridiculous...and excruciatingly painful. I spent hours in traction and thirty years suffering from neck pain. When I'd wake up in the morning towards the latter stages of these whiplash injuries, my hands would be numb. I couldn't hold a coffee cup or toothbrush for ten minutes after I awoke...then feeling would come back and I'd be ok. It was getting to be continuous, and a doctor told me that if my hands stayed numb for over twenty minutes, I would have to have surgery that week or face permanent nerve damage. So, I started to look for a neurosurgeon who could perform the surgery, not IF that happened, but WHEN. After five different interviews I found the doctor I felt comfortable with doing the surgery WHEN it was necessary— Frank Cammisa at a Hospital for Special Surgery in New York City.

Why I put this story in this epilogue is that I never have had the surgery. I took up golf and have not had neck pain since. I'm sure many people with sore backs have been told to give up golf, but for me and my kind of injury, golf was just the therapy needed to loosen up my neck and keep it loose. If I go a couple weeks without hitting a golf ball, my neck starts to tighten up again, my hands get numb, and I'm in pain.

So, see? Golf for me has created many benefits. I love the friends I've made on the golf course. Tom and I get to travel to many great golf courses (Tom's of course— over 300). We spend many hours TOGETHER doing something we both enjoy and can talk about later.

I get to be in nature enjoying the flora and fauna. There's an Egyptian geese pair who have ten babies this year at Jupiter hills golf course. All of my girlfriends and I have celebrated how the whole family is still intact...I've even painted a picture of them. We have eagles and osprey and pelicans that we watch dive into the waters at Jupiter hills and scoop out a fish—marvelous! I've watched seals in Pebble Beach while I was playing golf. Nature takes your breath away if you're in it for very long. In North Carolina, we've seen many mothers bears and their babies play on the golf course while we just sit back in amazement. The gentle kindness of the people who work at the courses we belong to makes my heart smile. I get involved in their lives— celebrate their joys and weep with their struggles.

The events at the golf course we belong to include dancing—where else except for weddings do we get the opportunities to dance? With your girlfriends (after we wear the guys out!). Where else can you find grown women in identical outfits to celebrate they are a TEAM...? When my son died four years ago, it was my golf girlfriends who kept me going. There's lots of reasons to take up this game, and I'm sure other sports can boast similar attributes that make them worth experiencing. But GOLF is the only sport that you can still play at 80/90 years old and still play competitively because of the handicap system.

And the golden cloud of taking up golf later in life is that I'm always getting better (so I'm still celebrating bogies) and long-time players are mad at themselves at their bogies. Also, it's taught me to be kinder to myself. My rule is to treat myself like my best friend. I wouldn't say to my best friend "you stupid idiot" so why would I say that to myself?

So, you see? I'm sold and I hope I've sold the game to you! I hope you'll read ALL of Bob Rotella's books. I hope you get to meet some of the heroes of the game that I have— Brad Faxon, Nancy Lopez, Billy Andrade, Michelle McGann— I'm in awe of them all because they love the game and have committed to playing it well. I'm so grateful to have been able to play so many wonderful courses. Augusta Country Club, Pebble Beach, Cypress Point...history you can feel that oozes up out of the ground and whispers from the trees...I'm so lucky.

The round is over, but the day isn't. We sling our bags a little lighter, scuff a tee into a pocket, and start the slow walk back—sun on our shoulders, wind tugging at the visor, shoes clicking on the path that's seen all our moods.

We don't talk about every shot. We don't have to. The game is already fading into the soft blur it deserves: a pure 7-iron that felt like silk; the bunker that tried to make us cry; the chip that cozied up to the flag and made us feel like geniuses for a whole minute. One of us is replaying a miss; another is already ordering French fries in her head. Someone says, "Next time," and we all nod, because that's the spell golf casts—there is always a next time.

This is the part I didn't know I needed: the after. The small mercy of walking side by side when the scorecard is folded away and the pressure has slipped off our backs like a rain jacket. We notice the color of the sky. We notice each other. We tell the truth in little pieces—about the putt, about our kids, about the thing that was heavier than our bags when we teed off. We laugh at nothing and everything. If a cartwheel almost happened on 17, it's definitely happening in the retelling now.

At the clubhouse door, there's the familiar chorus—ice clinking, girls congratulating another gal for her birdie on 18, saying how good that long putt was on hole 14, someone clapping for a long one that actually dropped. We hand the card to the table, not like a report card but like a postcard: Wish you were here. Sometimes we add it up; sometimes the trash can is the holiest place in the room. Either way, we count what matters: one brave swing when it would've been easier to pick up, one kind word that softened a friend's shoulders, one breath that steadied a shaking thumb. Grace, grit, girlfriends—tallied and under par.

Golf has taught me a tender kind of courage. Not the drum-beating kind, but the everyday kind: try again, breathe again, show up again. Keep your head still and your heart soft. Aim for a tiny spot and let the big things— love, laughter, forgiveness—do their wide, generous work.

Before we leave, we promise each other the same things we promised the ball: we'll be back; we'll keep it simple; we'll remember to have fun. We'll fix our divots out there and a few of the ones we make in life, too. We'll carry what is ours to carry and set down what isn't. And when the game exposes us, as it always does, we'll meet it with a smile that says, I can do hard things and make friends doing them.

Outside, the light is softer. We walk to our cars a little taller than we arrived—not because we played perfectly, but because we played at all. Because we chose wonder over worry, progress over pride, and each other over everything.

If today was your first round, I hope it isn't your last. If it was your worst, I hope you come back anyway. If it was your best, I hope you share your fries.

The course will be here tomorrow—green and stubborn and full of chances. So will we. Meet me on the tee. Same laugh. New ball. Let's go find all the next times.

Oh, in case you are thinking I must've become a scratch golfer with all of this practice and am writing a book to tell you that you too can become a scratch golfer at 75—NOPE—my lowest index has been a 13 and is now 16.4...and I'm still LOVING the game—the challenge— and my GIRLFRIENDS!

FAZIOS CELEBRATION, June 2025